SMALL BRAND AMERICA V

Special Bourbon Edition

BY
STEVE AKLEY

Written and Published by:
Steve Akley

To my fellow "Bourbon Heads":

If you love bourbon as much as I do, you are going to enjoy this look "behind the barrels" to learn a little more about these fascinating companies and the people who own them!

Small Brand America V
Special Bourbon Edition

Preface

My only goal when I began writing was to simply write about what I liked. Stating this, it sounds like some sort of ego driven charge, but I can assure you it is not.

This really isn't an assertion of "This is what I write Mr. or Ms. Reader, so you are going to read it." Actually, it's a deeper understanding of potential readers and a contrite self-assessment of my own skills. I have full understanding of the fact the only way my passion as a writer comes through is if I am completely interested in a topic.

With this in mind, **Small Brand America V** should be my greatest book I've ever written. My own passion project.

You see, I am a bourbon fan. A mega bourbon fan. I love everything about bourbon from the history, the process of creating it, the small brands, the large brands, the bottles, the labels.

All of it!

I have toured distilleries from small, one person operations, to the Bourbon Trail in Kentucky, showcasing the largest brands in the industry. My personal stash of bourbon never falls below 50 bottles at any given time. It's an evolving collection with a few favorites always present and other rotated in and out as I attempt to be "the guy" who discovers new brands to introduce to my friends. During the holidays I'm constantly fielding calls with comments like, "Okay, I'm going to a party. They aren't big bourbon drinkers so I want something really smooth" or "I'm buying a gift for a true bourbon aficionado I want to impress." I get their budget and make a few recommendations.

There isn't a greater joy in the world of retail for me than shopping the bourbon section at a store. All of those offerings, each trying to grab your attention, trying to jump off of the shelf. Just staring at the colors from amber-yellow to smoky-brown is intoxicating. My wife doesn't get why I need to stand in front of all of these bottles just staring. Seemingly hypnotized. You have to take it in, though. About three feet back and just stare. (Trust me, it works.)

Despite the potential to do so, I'm not getting too technical with this topic. If a bottle says bourbon, and the company being featured actually made it without outsourcing their production to a larger distiller, I wanted to speak to them.

You see, the term "bourbon" can even be a little complicated.

For starters, what I love is bourbon represents a uniquely "Made in America" product. Seemingly perfect for a series of books entitled, **Small Brand America**, right?

At the macro level the term bourbon carries three stipulations:
1). It's produced in the United States (as stated before, I like that one).
2). It's made from a grain mixture of at least 51% corn.
3). It's aged in new, charred oak barrels.

The other macro stipulations get a little technical. Proofing at distilling, going into the barrel and bottled. You can even get further into the weeds with terms like "bourbon" versus "straight bourbon."

These are Federal guidelines which differ state-by-state. I'm not saying these technicalities and terms do not matter. They absolutely do and impact what is in the bottle, and perhaps the informed consumers want to really complete an assessment of the potential brands or bottles they are buying.

My only point here is that, I, as an author, didn't want to set some standards as to what I thought the term bourbon meant and then hold the companies I was featuring to my personal definition.

There were only two parameters for eligibility to be in the book:
1). The company sells a bourbon they actually produce.
2). They have bourbon on the label. I realize this can vary depending on where they are producing the product, but so long as they have gone through the eligibility requirements of the state they are manufacturing in, I'm good with that.

Of course, what goes without saying is they have to be a small brand. That, too, is a little loose, but my personal definition would be any company other than the dozen or so megabrands found in the loop of the Bourbon Trail in Kentucky is eligible.

Not only does each have a little bit of a different take on how they make their bourbon, the personal stories of the people behind the brands are fascinating. Do yourself a favor. Before you even start reading about the companies, get yourself some bourbon because you are going to crave it once you begin reading, anyway. I don't know why, but it's true. It happened to me while writing, and to my editors and early edition readers.

The next time you are out shopping, carve out some time to shop the bourbon section. Three feet back. Stare. First scanning the section, then let your eyes deep focus to the point of being out of focus. Almost like you are looking at some of that 3-D art they used to sell at the mall. This will ensure you find the right bourbon for your own consumption.

Also, be sure to seek out the brands in the book. Their passion and dedication comes through in the pages here, but the taste of their product does not. For that, there is no substitute to glass in hand. Neat, please! So be sure to pick up a bottle if you see their product on your favorite store's shelves.

After all, each one represents **Small Brand America**!

Table of Contents

Chapter 1
2bar Spirits

2bar
SPIRITS

2960 4th Avenue South
Seattle, WA 98134
(206) 402-4340

2barspirits.com
info@2barspirits.com

Established
2010

Leadership
Nathan Kaiser, Owner

Product Lineup:
Bourbon(s)
2bar Bourbon Whiskey

Other
Vodka & Moonshine

"You always have to be careful with quality because no matter what your size is this business is still about volume."
     -Nathan Kaiser

If you have seen the movie *Social Network*, starring Jessie Eisenberg, you've seen how crazy it can get in the world of tech startups. Whether the movie was actually true, or simply a Hollywood version of the truth, the world of technology does, in fact, evolve quickly, often resulting in financial windfalls for the stakeholders of these companies.

Nathan Kaiser lived the "*Social Network* lifestyle" for most of the late 1990s and early 2000s before starting 2bar Spirits in 2010. "Okay," you're probably thinking, "I know what happens here, Nathan hit it big in the world of technology now he's looking for something to do with the mountain of cash he's sitting on."

Well, it easily could be the story here, but it's not.

Nathan owned a few tech start-ups himself, as well as being part of multiple companies as a consultant. He had the talent and skills to be successful. Also, he certainly was involved in enough businesses to take a chance at hitting one of those homeruns which ends up being a financial windfall, but, he kind of *struck out*… at least from the Mark Zuckerberg uber-billionaire perspective.

Then again, during this time in his life, Nathan wasn't measuring success with stock options, corporate buyouts and IPOs. The travels, crisscrossing the country from his home state of Texas to New York to the Pacific Northwest, resulted in more opportunities to meet girls. Seemingly more beautiful girls with each new relocation.

Now, that's success!

The greatest financial windfall Nathan received from any of the multitude of companies he was involved in was a $6,000 bonus. Not long after receiving his check, he got a note from the IRS stating the company hadn't properly reported his payout so he ended up paying it back.

(Insert Pac-Man dying noise in your head to designate failure here.)

As Nathan reflects on his time as a tech mogul, he doesn't actually view it as a failure, though. He learned much about business and in his final stop in Seattle he met the woman he would marry.

(Insert Beethoven's *Ode to Joy* in your head here to designate triumph.)

Getting married and having children meant Nathan needed something much more stable in terms of employment and income. Nathan liked the idea of selling a product instead of a service as he had been doing with tech. After graduating with a microbiology degree, he had sold medical equipment and preferred the idea of selling a tangible product, and, in particular, something he was making himself.

As an avid whiskey drinker, he started researching the idea of opening a distillery. As he spoke with family and friends, he learned he had a family history making whiskey, albeit illegal moonshining, but a history nonetheless.

For five generations in South Texas, his family has run a ranch called 2bar. The 2bar Ranch is well-known in the area about 90 minutes south of Austin. Nathan's grandfather still runs the ranch today, and it was he who told Nathan that Nathan's great-grandfather had actually done some moonshining "back in the day" in addition to the legitimate ranching for which 2bar is so well-known.

That discussion was the only motivation Nathan needed to know the opportunity to open his own distillery was right for him. Plus, as a nod to his family heritage, he would name his company 2bar Spirits. Nathan raised the money he needed to get going from friends and family, and he started his distillery.

As a whiskey fan, he wanted bourbon to be the cornerstone of his product lineup. Of course, bourbon takes time to age, so he needed some products he could bring to market quickly. His plan was to produce both a vodka and an unaged whiskey (moonshine). He was thinking the popularity of vodka would result in a sales mix of about 95% vodka and about 5% moonshine. Much to his surprise, actual sales numbers were about equal for the two products. It was apparent 2bar had a whiskey-drinking clientele! This seemed like a great opportunity for a whiskey-maker who wanted to bring Washington's first state-produced bourbon to the market.

Nathan built his bourbon recipe backwards through trial and error. He knew the flavor profile he wanted; he just needed to figure out how to create it. His final mash bill consists of 55% corn rounded out with wheat and malted barley. One of the flavor enhancers he established in his process was a longer ferment time. Most companies are fermenting their mash bill from 48 – 96 hours. Nathan ferments his for two weeks.

This extra time gives Nathan a flavor profile of a butterscotch sweetness, and it brings out the wheat, as well. There are notes of vanilla and honey, and his bourbon finishes with dark chocolate and cherry undertones.

The tip-off that Nathan might have a whiskey-craving clientele based upon his strong moonshine sales numbers was right on. His customers love the strong, bold flavor of 2bar Bourbon Whiskey.

Despite the fact he's only selling in the State of Washington, he can't keep his product in stock. Currently, he's turning away retail outlets to focus on servicing the business he currently has.

In addition to his outstanding product offerings, the name 2bar has really connected with customers. With the trend of consumers looking to buy local, the onus is often on the company to tell the consumer why. "What's the story which sets you apart from the other companies out there, and what is the reason why I want to buy your product over a competitors?"

It's true.

Today's educated consumers don't just buy product, they buy the story of the company and the person behind the brand. 2bar is not only the name of Nathan's company, it's the entre into his personal story and a symbol of his family's history.

Visiting 2bar is an experience reminiscent of a South Texas ranch. It's a "modern rustic" décor. There are photos of the actual 2bar Ranch throughout the interior. The production facility is viewable behind a sliding glass door. Consumers can sample and purchase product right onsite, as well.

For Nathan, the best part of owning 2bar Spirits is seeing how consumers have taken ownership of the company. He loves seeing photos posted on social media of people talking about how it's not a party without a bottle, or bottles, of 2bar Spirits.

A recent investment in a new still has doubled production output while reducing production time for 2bar from 24 hours a day down to an 8 – 9 hour day. Nathan wants to grow the company but at a manageable rate, which doesn't hurt quality. In the long-term, he would like to grow regionally and see where it goes from there; but for the near-term, he's simply focusing on the State of Washington.

Despite all of their success and demand, 2bar is still only being sold in approximately 2% of retailers in the state. Nathan foresees spending the next 2 – 4 years conquering his "backyard" before he seeks opportunities elsewhere.

Take that Mark Zuckerberg!

2bar Spirits Photo Album

Nathan Kaiser

Inside 2bar Spirits

The "2bar" logo is right from Nathan's family's 2bar Ranch in South Texas

Nathan's grandfather and father at the ranch

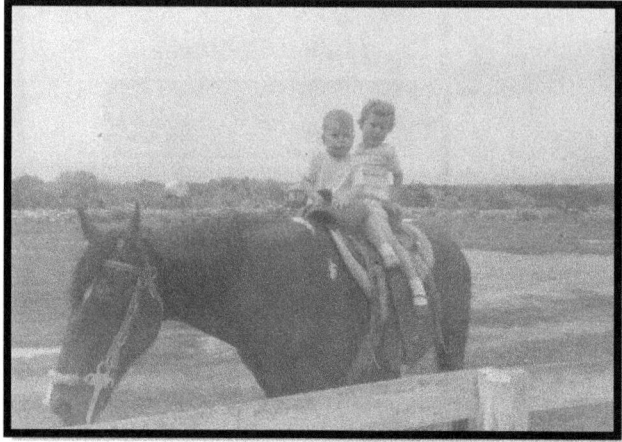

Having fun at the ranch

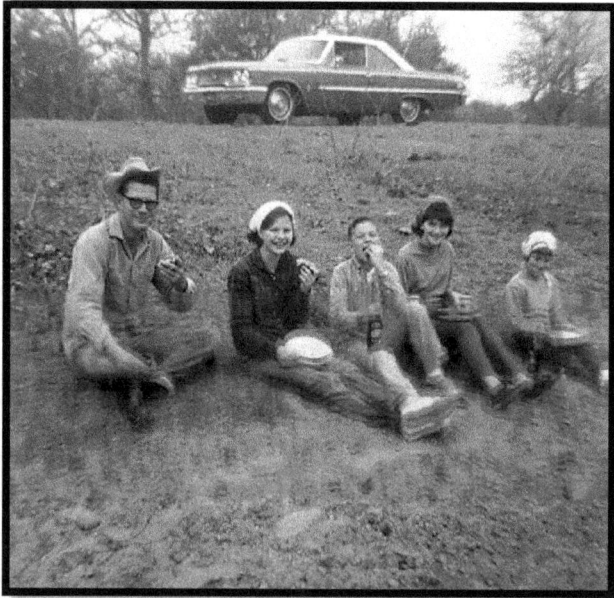

Family picnic at the ranch, 1967

The pasture at the 2bar Ranch today

2bar Spirits Bourbon Whiskey

Chapter 2

10th Mountain Whiskey & Spirit Company

286 Bridge Street
Vail, CO 81657
(970) 470-4215

10thwhiskey.com
ryan@10thwhiskey.com or christian@10thwhiskey.com

Established
2014

Leadership
Christian Avignon & Ryan Thompson, Co-Founders

Product Lineup:
Bourbon(s)
10th Mountain Whiskey & Spirit Company Bourbon

Other
Moonshine, Whiskey, Vodka and a Cordial

"We're more than a whiskey company. We're a mountain lifestyle brand."
-Ryan Thompson

Dwight D. Eisenhower once stated, "History does not long entrust the care of freedom to the weak or timid." It's easy for those of us who enjoy binge TV watching, playing fantasy football, sipping $7 lattes and checking our online 401(k) allocations to forget exactly what the cost of our freedom has been through the course of history and continuing today.

Unlike most, friends Ryan Thompson and Christian Avignon never have been the types to take their freedom for granted. In fact, they not only pledged never to forget the sacrifice of so many men and women for their freedom, they've made it a joint mission to promote the heroic efforts of an Army division both of them feel a special and personal bond with.

Ryan Thompson grew up in Texas. Ryan's favorite week of the year was the week his family would spend vacationing and skiing in Vail, Colorado. After graduating Southern Methodist University, he moved to Vail to live there full-time. He started out bartending to make ends meet. As he worked at the bar, he began to understand the business side of running a restaurant.

Thinking he may one day like to open a restaurant, he found himself evaluating dining establishments when he visited. There was always one restaurant in particular he believed wasn't living up to its potential. He felt there was a lot of upside, but the owners just weren't running it in a manner to maximize its capabilities.

When the restaurant came up for sale in 2002, it seemed like fate, so Ryan bought it. His assessment of the potential for the restaurant had been correct. He renamed it the Westside Cafe, updated the interior, reworked the menu, began marketing it, and the establishment quickly turned around and became profitable.

Christian Avignon was also a transplant to Vail looking to find his place in the area by starting a business. Christian had grown up in upstate New York, but moved to Vail at the encouragement of his grandfather. His grandfather, a World War II veteran, sang the praises of the beauty, serenity and fun of the area for a single young man like Christian.

Christian's grandfather had served in the 10th Mountain Division of the U.S. Army just outside of Vail. The unit came about in response to fighting in Europe where some of the enemy had been able to traverse and fight utilizing skis in the mountainous regions of the area. This Army infantry unit had success in some notable battles during World War II, any number of which could have turned the tide of the war had the 10th Mountain unit not been successful.

It's hard to believe now, but back in the 1940s, there wasn't the skiing culture we have in the U.S. today. This was true even in a place where we now almost solely associate with skiing like Vail, Colorado. When these soldiers came back from WWII, many settled in Vail and the surrounding areas, bringing the concept of a ski culture with them. In fact, after World War II, 62 ski resorts, ski schools and ski patrols were started by individuals who had served the U.S. Army in the 10th Mountain Division. They literally created an industry in the United States.

While Christian's grandfather went back to upstate New York following the war, he had always loved and yearned for the area around Vail, Colorado. With Christian not having a set path or career in New York, he opened the young man's eyes to what would await him if he made the move to the Centennial State.

Christian followed his grandfather's advice and made the move to Vail where he found work in the construction industry. Before long, he started his own business, Avignon Stone and Outdoor Living. He quickly became one of the area's most successful masonry companies.

Ryan and Christian met around 1999 while skiing. They were taking a break in the bar and began talking while enjoying a few beers. They seemed to have a lot in common. They were about the same age, and both had a desire to own their own business (they had not yet started their respective companies). The friendship, which started over those beers at the ski lodge, lasted as they ultimately started their own businesses in two distinctively different fields.

As both of their businesses became successful, the friends began to bounce ideas off one another of something they could do together. When they got information for a class called Moonshine University in Kentucky, they decided to attend together to learn the business and explore if it was feasible to open a distillery together in Vail.

After learning the process and the science of distilling, they were ready to move forward with starting a jointly-owned business. Their individual strengths, Ryan knowing the food and beverage industry, and Christian's knowing the construction side, seemed to meld well together in starting a distillery.

The name for their company was an obvious one: 10th Mountain Whiskey & Spirit Company. After all, they felt like everything from their freedom to the love of what they like doing in their spare time (skiing in Colorado) was a result of the brave men who had served their country in this unit. With the help of Christian's grandfather's connections, they were able to ensure the 10th Mountain Unit felt as positive about being honored in this manner as they did about doing it. They were pleased to find enthusiasm from members of 10th Mountain. The consensus from past and present members (the unit is still active now training in Fort Drum, New York) was that it was an honor to be recognized with the name as well as to introduce the division's heroism and role in American history to others.

In addition to their training at Moonshine University, Christian and Ryan worked with a master distiller to refine their approach and recipes. They developed a bourbon which should deliver a sweeter profile than what is typically found on the market under the megabrand labels. "Should" being key there since they are a start-up company, and bourbon takes time to mature. They are in the process of aging it right now. Ryan points out, "The bourbon will tell you when it's ready."

In the meantime, they have released a young bourbon. It's been aged 6 months, and the response to this initial offering has been very positive. At the six month mark, this bourbon, made up of 75% corn, is already delivering that sweet taste Ryan and Christian were looking for.

It's safe to say life is going pretty well for Ryan Thompson and Christian Avignon. The Westside Cafe and Avignon Stone and Outdoor Living, Ryan and Christian's respective businesses, continue to succeed. 10th Mountain continues to exceed expectations. They currently have a mountain-rustic-style tasting room in downtown Vail, offering a virtual tour. In nearby Gypsum, Colorado, they have a 7,000 square foot facility where individuals can see production firsthand, enjoy their tasting room and even rent it for private events like wedding receptions and corporate events.

Currently, their product is available locally around Vail via self-distribution, but Ryan and Christian are going to begin working with a distributor, and their product will be available around the State of Colorado very soon. The ultimate goal for distribution is to get their "American-made/American-proud" product available in all fifty states.

They have to be careful in managing this planned growth, though, because their product doesn't just represent a distilled spirits company; it's a reflection of something they both respect and hold "near and dear," and that's the soldiers of the 10th Mountain Division. In addition, Ryan and Christian contribute a portion of all of their sales to three charities:
1). **The Vail Veterans** program, helping veterans locally.
2). **The 10th Foundation,** helping individuals in need who have served under their namesake unit.
3). **The Wounded Warrior Program,** which helps assist active duty military members who are injured in the line of duty as they return home.

Revenue growth charts with arrows pointing upwards are often the ultimate affirmation of how well a business is doing. For Ryan Thompson and Christian Avignon it may run a little deeper than that. Sure, profitability remains their ultimate goal, but sometimes in life there are little reminders pointing to the fact there are things that may be even more important.

A friend of Lt. General Bill Carpenter was on a trip to Vail and saw what Ryan and Christian were doing with their company. For those of you who don't know Lt. General Carpenter, his bio reads like something you would see put together for a G.I. Joe action figure. This Army legend is a College Football Hall of Famer for his career as a defensive end on the Army football team. His combat action in Vietnam earned him both the Silver Star and Distinguished Service Cross. He capped his military career by commanding the 10th Mountain Division for the last 20 years of his military service.

Shortly after the friend of Lt. General Carpenter visited, they received an autographed photo which was inscribed, "Great Soldiers, Great Division, Great Booze!"

There is a lot to love about what Ryan and Christian are doing. In fact, it's almost comforting to see that two men are doing so well with a business which has a quality product while not only recognizing the efforts of our nation's heroes but takes it a step further by supporting charities dedicated to the men and women of the U.S. Armed Forces.

Still, for Ryan and Christian, there is no higher honor than the positive attestation Lt. General Carpenter gave to them with the autographed photo.

Cheers to Ryan, Christian, the soldiers of the 10th Mountain as well as all who serve, and have served, in the U.S. Military!

10th Mountain Photo Album

Christian Avignon & Ryan Thompson

10th Mountain's marketing is reflective of their dedication to the "mountain lifestyle"

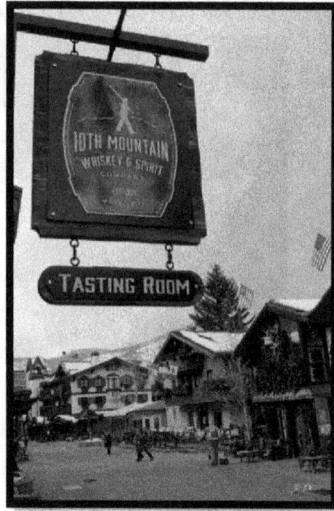

Outside of the tasting room

Inside of the Tasting Room

Use Christian and Ryan for scale here

Barrels lined up

10th Mountain Whiskey & Spirit Company product lineup

Chapter 3
Barrel House Distilling Co.

Barrel House Distilling Co.
1200 Manchester Street, Building #9
Lexington, KY 40504
(859) 259-0159

barrelhousedistillery.com
barrelhousedistillery@yahoo.com

Established
2008

Leadership
Jeff Wiseman & Peter Wright, Co-Owners

Product Lineup:
Bourbon(s)
Barrel House Distilling Co. Bourbon

Other
Vodka, Rum and Moonshine

"We are in Kentucky, the epicenter of bourbon production for the world."
-Jeff Wiseman

After selling an air freight business he had owned for 20 years, Jeff Wiseman began seeking his next adventure. In the time after the sale of his business, he had been flipping houses to fulfill his creative energy and earn some extra income. Still, he knew it wasn't a long-term solution.

On a "guys' weekend" in Florida over more than a few bourbons, he and his buddy Peter Wright, a neurologist specializing in pain management, began talking about the distilled spirits industry. They had grown up on the same street and had been buddies since grade school. Both were confirmed bourbon aficionados. The knowledge and respect they had for the whiskey business meant they were well-versed in the industry. They spoke of how Kentucky had once been home to more than 2,000 distilleries before Prohibition. At the time of their trip, there were only 8 distilleries in Kentucky, and these were all of the largest and most well-known names in the bourbon business.

The local/craft whiskey companies, which had been a hallmark of the area, were now all gone. The conversation turned to the idea of entering the market as a craft distiller. The laws had begun to change in favor of the artisanal producer of fine distilled spirits, and it seemed to make perfect sense, even for two guys with absolutely no distilling experience, to enter the market.

While most Florida guys' weekend conversations are best kept in Florida, this one picked back up when they returned to Kentucky. Even fully sober, the plan Jeff and Peter had started on their trip still seemed idyllic.

Together, they wrote a business plan, and, from an outsider's perspective, their formal training seemed more like an expanded version of a Florida guys' weekend trip. Jeff and Peter actually traveled to multiple distilleries across the United States, learning the process of making distilled spirits and meeting the individuals behind them. They were extremely pleased to find the support of not only distilleries outside of their market, but even several of the 8 largest distilleries domiciled in Kentucky.

You would think the only goal of these large companies would be to crush a small start-up, but Jeff and Peter found the opposite to be true. There is a recognition from both the individual companies, as well as through the Kentucky Distillers' Association, of the relevance of craft distillers. Both entities recognize the fact the growth of craft distillers is more than a fad, and if Kentucky wants to maintain its role as the center of bourbon production, all parties need to embrace and support the small distilleries.

Jeff and Peter selected a name for their company and began seeking a home for their business when an unbelievable stroke of good luck was bestowed upon them. The old site of the James E. Pepper distillery had just been purchased by a developer. He was going to turn it into a destination site with restaurants and entertainment venues appealing to locals and tourists.

James E. Pepper was a distillery started in 1780 in Lexington, Kentucky. In the 1800s they moved from the location where Woodford Reserve resides today to the location the developer had just purchased. Over time, the company expanded into multiple buildings on a grand scale to accommodate the large volume of product they were producing. (For instance, the Aging House building was five stories tall and had a footprint of 250,000 square feet.)

James Pepper, the person behind the brand, was a legend in the industry having invented the grandfather of all bourbon cocktails, the Old Fashioned. The company even managed to survive Prohibition as a medicinal whiskey production facility.

Still, despite all of the success, and a run of over 175 years, eventually, the company fell on hard times. The factory was closed for good in 1958. It sat empty for 50 years until being purchased by the developer. After Jeff and Peter met with him, they moved forward with purchasing the Barrel House building on the James E. Pepper site to house their company. The next step Jeff and Peter took was to change the name from what they had planned to Barrel House Distilling Co. as a nod to the unique bourbon history they were buying into.

The good luck of being able to land such a historic building has really had a positive impact on what Jeff and Peter are doing. Bourbon has such a strong following that individuals began seeking them to visit their company and learn a little more about the history of the site. When the Kentucky Distillers' Association incorporated a Craft Tour leg into their famous Bourbon Trail, they added Barrel House Distilling Co. to the list. At the kickoff event, it was amazing for Jeff and Peter to see such bourbon legends as Jimmy Russell, the master distiller of Wild Turkey, and Chris Morris from Woodford Reserve in attendance.

The status of being amongst a handful of companies on the Craft Tour of the Bourbon Trail has opened the company to a large audience. In 2012, for instance, they had over 12,000 visitors representing all 50 states and 9 countries. Jeff and Peter bring people back time-after-time because they do not have a set tour. They talk about what's going on that day, which can vary greatly depending on what they are making, or doing, at the factory. Since tours aren't rehearsed, it's often the guests setting the direction as to what happens during a visit.

As an active member of the Kentucky Distillers' Association, Jeff Wiseman notes that many of the members have thanked him as the craft distillers have helped redistribute the crowds amongst more distilleries since the large companies had been getting overwhelmed during peak visitation months.

Of course, a great facility, having the support of the larger competitors and even being part of the Bourbon Trail, is only a portion of the reason Barrel House Distilling Co. has been such a success. Without an outstanding product, all this goodwill would be quickly washed away.

Luckily, Jeff and Peter back up everything they have working in their favor with a stellar bourbon offering. The grain they utilize is grown locally and stone ground at a local mill. They create a wheated bourbon with a double distillation process through a 500 liter hand-hammered pot still. Currently, they use barrels ranging in size from 15 – 53 gallons but are transitioning to the larger barrels based largely upon the high cost of the smaller barrels (about twice the cost of the larger barrels).

The site of the old James E. Pepper Distillery, now known as the Distillery District, is thriving. Not only is Barrel House Distilling Co. bringing crowds, there are restaurants, a brewery and a multitude of entertainment venues. Jeff and Peter note they have plenty of room to grow in their current venue but never plan to get too big so that their quality begins to suffer. They recognize the fact they have plenty of opportunity to grow and still maintain their status as a small craft distiller.

Perhaps taking all of this into consideration, it might not be surprising that despite all of the success and thrills Jeff and Peter have experienced with Barrel House Distilling since opening in 2008, Jeff quickly notes the best part of doing what he is doing now is simply walking into his business each morning and smelling the mash.

Isn't it awesome the answer isn't a reiteration of a business plan or a canned corporate response? Sounds like a person who simply loves what he is doing. A true passion for the product he is producing.

Then again, would you expect any other answer from a bourbon aficionado who sketched out his idea for his business during a guys' weekend in Florida?

Barrel House Distilling Co. Photo Album

Paul Wright & Jeff Wiseman

The Tasting Room at Barrel House Distilling

Being on the Craft Tour of the Bourbon Trail has been a key marketing strategy for Barrel House Distilling

The still

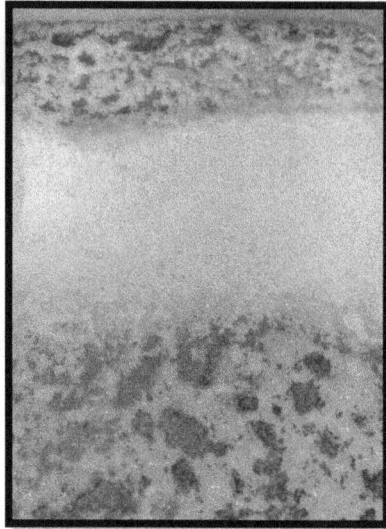

Mash

Filling a barrel

Barrels aging

Is it bourbon, yet?

Chapter 4
Black Dirt Distillery

BLACKDIRTDISTILLERY.COM

Pine Island, NY
(845) 216-6900

blackdirtdistillery.com
info@blackdirtdistillery.com

Warwick Winery: 114 Little York Road, Warwick, NY 10990

Established
2012

Leadership
Jeremy Kidde & Jason Grizzanti, Co-Founders & Managing Partners

Product Lineup:
Bourbon(s)
Black Dirt Bourbon & Black Dirt Single Barrel Bourbon

Other
Applejack

"You become an entrepreneur thinking the only goal to running a business is to make money. You quickly find out that it is only one component of the satisfaction you get in running a company."
   -Jeremy Kidde

Rarely do plans formulated through the youthful eyes of high schoolers come to fruition. It's certainly understandable how changes might occur. The exuberance of "my whole life is ahead of me" causes many of us to consider different scenarios as we begin to forge our own path. The very process of the self-examination needed to determine which direction we go in adulthood means most of those youthful plans get cast aside and never looked back on again.

Buddies Jeremy Kidde and Jason Grizzanti looked at one scenario as they were starting to work on their own career plans. In 1994, Jason's father, a doctor, had started a business on a farm he purchased. For Jason's father, it represented a small, but diversified business (it would become a working orchard, winery and distillery) he could manage working as a physician while envisioning it as his retirement job.

High school students Jeremy and Jason saw some opportunities with Jason's father's business. Because Jason's father didn't have the time to devote his full attention to it, they felt perhaps they could partner up to expand Warwick Valley Winery and Distillery beyond being a small local provider of wine and hard cider.

It appeared their plans would be forever tossed aside as both went other directions as they headed off to college. Ultimately, Jeremy felt the corporate life would be the path for him. He went to college in Maine and landed a great job in banking which took him out west to San Francisco. Jason also went in a totally different direction. He went to Cornell and got a science degree. As his undergraduate work wrapped up, he started making plans to go to law school.

While Jason was helping out his father back at the farm, still deciding on where he wanted to go to law school, tragedy struck the family of his old friend Jeremy Kidde. In 2001, Jeremy's father passed away. This brought Jeremy right back to the evaluation process most of us leave behind forever in high school. He knew he wanted to get back East to where his family was. Suddenly, career growth, as measured through rungs on a corporate ladder, didn't seem to matter anymore. He simply wanted to get back home.

In speaking with Jason, it was as if they just picked up where they left off so many years before. Neither of them had ever "cast aside" the idea of running the family farm. Both had just put it on the back burner for a while. With Jason questioning whether or not he wanted to move forward with law school, and Jeremy wanting to get back home to New York, the time was right for both of them to focus their full attention on the plan they had started working on in high school.

The first idea they came up with for changing the business from a small local provider to a bigger company was to build a brand. They felt it would be a difficult path with wine, but Jason and Jeremy were sure they had something special with the hard cider they were producing. At the time there wasn't much of a hard cider market in the U.S., but it was very popular in Europe. In comparing their product to what was commercially available, Jeremy and Jason found theirs' tasted a little more balanced. It was also a little drier than some of the super-sweet offerings on the market.

As they began to focus their attention on building brand recognition with their cider, the U.S. market began to pick up. Today, hard cider drinks are popular offerings from trendy dance clubs to neighborhood bars. Jeremy and Jason have been able to capture some of that success for themselves, expanding their brand from a small, local producer to now being available in 25 states and international exporting, as well.

As they started to see success in gaining traction building their cider brand, Jeremy and Jason saw the value of starting a second brand they could build up and focus on large scale distribution. Part of the charm of the farm is it is a self-contained entity which serves as a small local provider of wine, hard cider and gin. Additionally, it is a place where you can pick apples and pears. They feared further expansion of the name and brand of Warwick Valley Winery and Distillery might take away of some of the charm of that brand.

With this in mind, Jeremy and Jason opened a second business, Black Dirt Distillery in 2012. The name comes from the rich soil in the area left by glaciers as they cut through the dirt during the ice age. The area had been a swampy mess but in the late 1890s and early 1900s, settlers built drainage ditches which allowed them to farm this nutrient rich soil.

One of Warwick Valley Winery's most popular offerings was its Black Dirt Red. Even though it had no connection to the area beyond a name (the grapes were not grown locally), those from the area loved the tribute to the unique history of the area, and visitors from outside of the Warwick Valley thought it sounded cool.

Knowing they wanted to build a distillery which utilized the greatest resource of the area, the nutrient rich soil, it seemed like a no-brainer for Jeremy and Jason to go with Black Dirt Distillery for their new venture.

Black Dirt's bourbon offerings are certainly reflective of this vision. They utilize an 80% corn mash bill with all of the corn coming from the area. That's right, 100% of the corn they use is an heirloom variety, and it grows in the unique black dirt which serves as their company's namesake. You can tell a difference, too. A bite into the corn grown in the "black dirt" makes you say, "It tastes like corn."

It's an intense experience!

Their bourbon is aged three years in full-sized barrels. The end result is taste which yields a cracked corn creaminess.

Currently, Jeremy and Jason are in the middle of their expansion plans. The opening of Black Dirt Distillery in 2012 in nearby Pine Island, New York, represented a whole new era for the company. Immediately, their production expanded by 20 – 30 times, but they still have a lot of work to do to get them exactly where they envision the company. Their next step is building out more space for barrel storage where they can expand their bourbon and whiskey offerings.

After that, they will work on visitor facilities at their new location: a tasting room, retail space and a tour. For now, Warwick Valley Winery and Distillery is their home base for visiting and tastings.

The goal to expand distribution is for 2017 to be the year when they see the payoff of the work they are doing now. That may seem far off to some, but these are bourbon distillers. They understand patience and putting together a plan for tactical and manageable growth.

While the story of Jeremy and Jason started with the concept of walking away from high school dreams to pursue different paths, consider this…

Jason's work in the field of science at Cornell gave him the perfect background to take the lead on production, and it's the role he has fallen into for both of their companies (Black Dirt and Warkwick Valley).

Conversely, Jeremy's time in business and banking is the right business mix to help the company reach its goals in the market. He handles all of distribution, sales and marketing.

Are these guys not telling the whole story? Was there a bigger, "master plan" which was always in the works?

Well, Jeremy and Jason aren't saying. They are humble enough to leave you thinking timing and perhaps some luck along the way got them to where they are today.

However they got to where they are now… it's working!

Black Dirt Distillery Photo Album

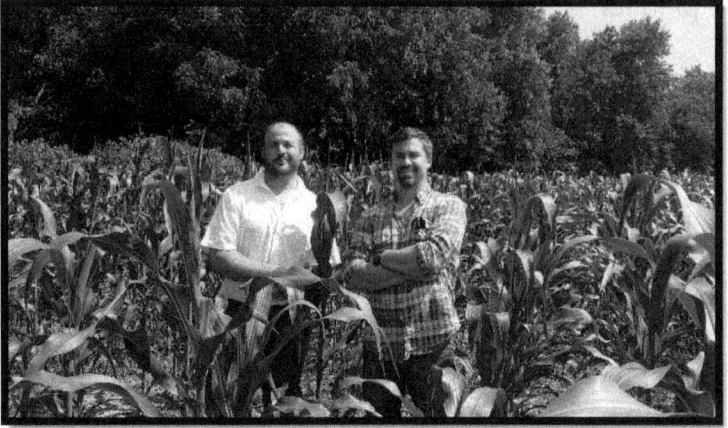

Jason Grizzanti & Jeremy Kidde

Black Dirt Distillery

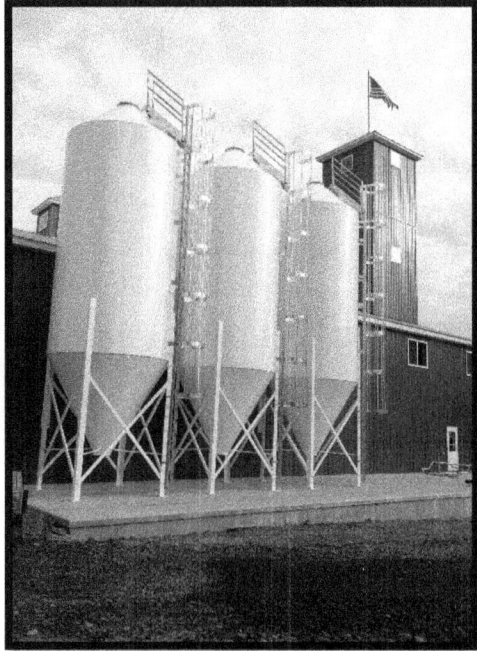

Grain bins (soon, this will be Black Dirt Bourbon!)

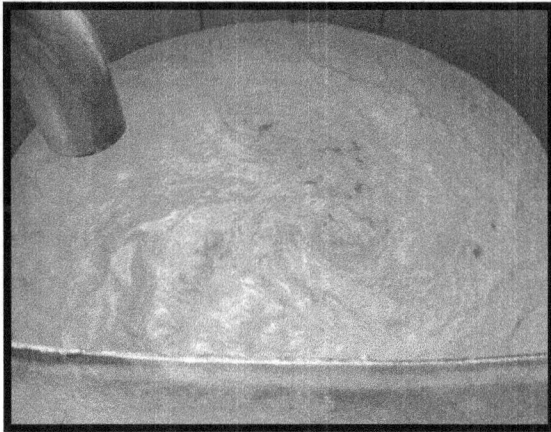

Mash

The still

Warwick Valley Winery & Distillery

Black Dirt's other offering beyond whiskey is Apple Jack

Black Dirt Bourbon

Chapter 5
Cedar Ridge Vineyards & Distillery

CEDAR RIDGE
DISTILLERY

1441 Marak Road NW
Swisher, IA 52338
(319) 857-4300

crwine.com
info@crwine.com

Established
2005

Leadership
Jeff & Laurie Quint, Proprietors
Jamie Siefken, General Manager

Product Lineup:
Bourbon(s)
Iowa Bourbon Whiskey
Reserve Bourbon
Port Cask Bourbon

Other
Wine, Brandy, Rum, Wheat Whiskey, Unaged Whiskey,
Single Malt Whiskey, Malted Rye Whiskey & Grappa

"I like the fact we create something we send out of state which showcases a product made in Iowa as well as one of our greatest resources here: Iowa corn."
  -Jamie Siefken

You don't have to know Jeff Quint personally to figure out that he's a "numbers guy." When you have both CPA and CFO after your name, like he does, it's always pretty safe to call that person a "numbers guy."

It was this love of numbers and finance, which led he and his wife Laurie to start their business. Yes, he and Laurie were actually hobby wine makers. Sure, Jeff had experienced distilling as a child, watching his dad experimenting at the house. Still, they were not the precursors for getting Cedar Ridge Vineyards and Distillery started.

It all began one day while he was taking a hard look at the finances and his future. (No doubt a 10-key calculator was involved.) As he made his calculations, he wasn't liking what he was seeing. He told Laurie he was simply never going to be able to retire. They needed to look for some other form of income they could perhaps manage now and turn their full attention to during their retirement.

Laurie, who had started dating Jeff in high school, knew her husband well. She knew that turning the discussion back to Jeff would be the best way to address his concerns. She turned to him and asked, "If you could do anything you want in retirement, what would you do?"

Jeff told Laurie he would like to live on a vineyard, making wine with cold climate grapes. Laurie liked the idea as well, and they explored starting a business. The numbers must have worked, since Jeff and Laurie ended up moving forward with the idea and purchasing a house with acreage.

In 2003, they planted their first grapes. Knowing it would take some time for the grapes to produce fruit, Jeff also decided to add distilling to the mix of his proposed business. He spent time in Germany in an apprenticeship, learning the artistry and science of distilling. Upon returning to Iowa, he began working with Iowa lawmakers to make his proposed new business legal. There hadn't been a distillery in Iowa since before Prohibition, and the local and state laws prohibited him from operating the new business he was planning.

After successfully lobbying for changes to the laws, he and Laurie were able to open their business, naming it after the beautiful area where their vineyards were planted in Swisher, Iowa, between Cedar Rapids and Iowa City. The area between the two, known as "The Corridor" is a flourishing part of Iowa. The growth of The Corridor has created a metropolis, which, when you include it with the population of Cedar Rapids and Iowa City, rivals Des Moines (Iowa's most populous city) in size.

Initially, Jeff and Laurie's business wasn't domiciled in Swisher, though. They couldn't afford the cost of building a working winery and distillery so they needed to find a more economically feasible way to start their business. They found a liquor store in downtown Cedar Rapids, Iowa, which offered the luxury of a production area in back and the ability to sell their product in front. Well, technically, it wasn't the Quints selling the product. The Quints were able to wholesale their product to the liquor store, who in-turn, could then sell it to the customers who were coming for a tasting of the offerings they were creating in the backroom.

For over three years, the Quints made this set-up work. Jeff and Laurie would work all day, Jeff as a CFO and Laurie as a teacher, and then they would go to the liquor store to produce their wines and distilled spirits. There, they would host tastings while Jeff was simultaneously producing product onsite.

When floods ravaged Cedar Rapids and their store in 2008, the Quints were not interested in rebuilding in the back of a liquor store. Instead, they began working on their own stand-alone location in Swisher, amongst the cold weather grapes they had planted.

Jeff's strong attention to detail, witnessed in his work in the financial world, has also manifested itself into his distilling business with great payoffs for his customers.

A perfect example can be seen in his bourbon production. In distilling spirits, master distillers control temperatures so they know exactly what is coming out of the still and when it's coming out. It's divided into three categories: Heads, Heart and Tails. The "Heads" represents the first 5% which comes out. It's filled with acetones and methylone. Even though these negatively impact taste, the big guys leave this in with the plans of letting the oak barrels and time mellow out those tastes.

Jeff siphons off that 5% from the "Heads" and discards it. His product never contains these harsh tasting bi-products of the distilling process. He only uses the 80% in middle of the distillation run, leaving the final 15%, "The Tails," to be run through the still again in another batch.

What Jeff is effectively doing in his process is using his still as a tool. He's controlling what his product tastes like by using it, but, ultimately, it's his creativity by controlling what goes into the barrels which then ends up in the bottles for his customers. The big guys are using their stills as the process. It's literally doing all of the work as whatever comes out is what goes into their barrels and, ultimately, into their bottles for their customers. It's a tiny tick of difference in approach, but if you think about it, you see how using the still as a tool can make a big difference.

The mash bill on their bourbon is 75% Iowa corn and the balance mixed between rye and barley creating a rye bourbon. They age their Iowa Bourbon Whiskey for two years and their Reserve Bourbon five years. The end result of using only the "Heart" of their distillation, and a rye mash bill featuring that famous Iowa corn, is an incredibly smooth-tasting product.

They also have a Port Cask Bourbon which they age for two years in oak barrels and then finish by aging it another year in a port wine cask. The port cask adds some light fruity taste to their bourbon with some mellow finishing notes.

Jeff and Laurie have excelled in creating a unique experience for guests visiting their facility. Despite the fact they are nestled right off the highway in Iowa between Iowa City and Cedar Rapids, someone looking around might feel more like they are no longer in the Midwest. Additional plantings in 2013 have brought the acreage to 47 in total now. The sprawling grape vines and trees are certainly reminiscent of an experience more likely found in California Wine Country than America's Heartland.

Inside, you get a rustic feel with a metal bar and concrete floors which is offset with a casual elegance of granite top tables. The entire experience is capped with a café style service throughout and a unique menu featuring creations by their three classically trained chefs on staff.

While Laurie has left her teaching job, Jeff continues to work as a chief financial officer and does secondary as Cedar Ridge's master distiller and master wine maker.

He's got plenty of help now, though. He has a management team which includes Kolin Brighton helping with production, Jamie Siefken serving as their general manager and his son Murphy handling wholesale and distribution.

Currently, they are building supply and inventory with plans to take their bourbon national. They are proud to be able to offer a product which highlights the fact Iowa is the largest corn producing state.

Retirement for Jeff?

No way!

Things are going way to well exactly as they are right now. Any good numbers guy will tell you that when things are going well, just keep doing what you are doing!

Cedar Ridge Vineyards & Distillery Photo Album

Jeff Quint

Cedar Ridge Distillery & Winery

The Tasting Room

Jamie Siefken, General Manager

Kolin Brighton, Production

Murphy Quint, Sales

Aging bourbon

Cedar Ridge's Reserve Bourbon Whiskey

Chapter 6
Colorado Gold Distillery

COLORADO Gold
ROCKY
MOUNTAIN WHISKEY

1290 South Grand Mesa Drive
Cedaredge, CO 81413
(970) 856-2600

coloradogolddistillers.com

Established
2007

Leadership
Peter Caciola, Owner
Mike Almy, Head Distiller

Product Lineup:
Bourbon(s)
Colorado Gold Straight Bourbon Whiskey

Other
Vodka, Hemp Vodka, Gin, Rye Whiskey, Corn Whiskey &
Agave

"Don't get in this business for the money. Get in because you have a passion for it. Everything else falls into place when you love what you do."
   -Mike Almy

Technically, the history of Colorado Gold Distillery goes back to 2007 when the company was founded. In reality, the company didn't start making history until Mike Almy joined the team in 2010. Prior to that, more often than not, they were struggling to stay afloat.

It's a good thing Mike made his way to Colorado Gold where he is leading the organization in an exciting new direction under the guidance of new owner Peter Caciola. Mike's path to Colorado Gold definitely was never a given. In fact, had things worked out better for him earlier in his career, he never would have thought about joining the company. It would take a struggling economy, a failed business attempt and a chance encounter to get him into the mix at Colorado Gold.

Colorado Gold Distillery was founded by Tom & Pam Cooper as a means to stay busy and earn income in retirement. Tom had retired from a 30+ year career in construction, and Pam had been a teacher for over 20 years. They liked the idea of getting into distilled spirits since it was a business model which could be effectively run by two people. Plus, Tom knew about distilling spirits from family back in Texas where he grew up. They had been moonshiners, and Tom knew the secrets of the trade from watching them.

Mike Almy graduated from Colorado State University with a degree in business. With the economy struggling in the early 2000s, he wasn't having any luck securing a job. Mike looked to his hobby when he couldn't find a job. Throughout college he had been a homebrewer, making his own beer. Additionally, he had worked at a liquor store to make ends meet while he went to school. Thinking a different career direction other than shopping around his business degree was in order, Mike took a chance and signed up for beer school. Mike felt some formal training to marry up with his interest from a hobby perspective could turn beer making into a career for him.

With the knowledge of crafting beer, as well as running a brewery gained from the beer school, Mike was ready to try his hand at running a craft brewery. He was able to secure four other investors who became equal partners with him.

Right out of the gate, Mike started to see the issues of running a business with five equal partners. For example, it took them three months to research and agree upon a name for their new business. Eventually, they agreed upon the name and started to slowly move forward in putting together their brewery. For two years they ground through the logistics of the business as well as waded through the legal processes on the local, state and federal levels to get a brewery going. Then, two of the owners decided they wanted out of the business. Cashing them out would have left the three remaining partners too cash-strapped to continue, so the group elected to pull the plug on their business before it ever really got started.

Mike had now come full circle to where he was when he graduated Colorado State University. He updated his résumé, and he started sought employment using his business degree. One of the first jobs he applied for was a position at a local bank.

On the job interview the person speaking to Mike reviewed his résumé. He told Mike, "No offense, but with your background, this isn't the job you should be applying for." That's usually not a real good sign in an interview.

The good news for Mike was the interviewer went on to explain that customers of the bank owned a distillery and were looking for help as they transitioned out of the business. He thought Mike might be a good fit to work at Colorado Gold Distillery with Tom and Pam Cooper.

Mike left the interview at the bank and headed to Colorado Gold to meet the Coopers. He quickly hit it off with them, but they explained they already had a distiller, pointing to a man working in the back of the building. They said the distiller was their only employee, and they couldn't bring anyone else onboard.

In yet another twist of fate, a few hours later Tom Cooper called Mike on the phone. The distiller, the Coopers' one employee, put in his two weeks' notice shortly after Mike had left. They actually could now use his help and hired him right then over the phone.

Though he hadn't distilled spirits before, the background in brewing was close enough that the transition was relatively easy for him. Mike trained alongside Tom for a year, and then he became the Head Distiller when Tom and Pam sold the business to Peter Caciola, a businessman from Texas.

Peter spent his entire career in the construction industry and currently owns his own flooring company. Distilled spirits was a business which always intrigued him. In fact, he had tried distilling on his own, but his marginal degree of success lead him to look to buy a business rather than try to start one himself.

Peter came into the business with the right approach. Rather than viewing Colorado Gold Distillery as an established business where he could look for revenue streams to pull out of it, he has taken a start-up approach by investing in the business. Since he has owned Colorado Gold, he has reinvested every penny of profit back into building his brand, increasing product offerings, building inventory and increasing capacity while maintaining quality.

One of the areas where Colorado Gold has always exceled was bourbon making. Simply put, the company was founded to be a bourbon manufacturer. The 6,500 foot elevation and dry climate make for unique aging of their bourbon. They currently age their bourbon three years in 53 gallon barrels. Each bottle is hand signed as a testament to Colorado Gold's hands-on approach in crafting their whiskey.

The flavor of the bourbon is unique. Like most craft distillers, it varies slightly from bottling-to-bottling based on the small batches they are making. One unique feature consistently noted by consumers is a hint of vanilla. The unique taste of Colorado Gold's bourbon led to a gold medal at the 2013 World Spirits Competition.

While bourbon may be the company's flagship product, their newest entry into the distilled spirts world may put the company on the map. In reading through the rules and regulations for the alcohol industry in the State of Colorado, the team at Colorado Gold noticed a clause had been added in 2001, allowing alcohol to be made of hemp (specifically vodka, which is typically made of grain or potatoes, but can be made of any plant-based matter containing starch or sugar). While it is highly likely a distillery had pushed for this addition (it seems unlikely lawmakers would have simply added this in on their own), none had actually brought a product to market.

Hemp, often associated with its cousin in the cannabis family, the marijuana plant, has one big difference. Its seeds don't produce the THC which causes the high. Still, because it is so closely associated with marijuana, hemp is classified as a Schedule I Drug by the U.S. government. What makes hemp unique, though, is the fact it isn't a drug, so you can legally import hemp.

The Colorado Gold team imports their hemp from Canada. They mix it with local grains to follow suit with their dedication of offering local products to their customers. The hemp must go through a testing process before production begins as well as a second round of testing after it has been made into vodka to ensure it doesn't have any trace of THC.

Of course, Colorado famously made the purchase of marijuana legal in 2014. Colorado Gold gives their own "wink-wink" to this fact by printing "Legalized 2014" on their labels which is accurate in describing the first hemp vodka offering in Colorado while subtly acknowledging the perceived connection between hemp and its much more famous cousin.

Currently, Colorado Gold's products can be found in 12 states. Owner Peter Caciola is going to make the ultimate investment back into his company by significantly increasing production by opening two new facilities. Their current location in Cedaredge, Colorado, doesn't have any ski resort traffic so they miss out on the rich tourism business found in their state.

The plan is to open up a small distillery in Denver. They will distill their whiskey at the Denver site which will open them up to Colorado's most populous city. There, they will not only have whiskey production in Denver but offer tours and a tasting room, as well.

In their second, much larger facility, in a yet to be determined Colorado city, they will craft their vodka, gin and other distilled spirits. The goal for the second site is to have placement in a city which does capture tourist traffic so a spot near a ski resort is their most likely destination.

Peter Caciola's business savvy and dedication to growing his company, combined with Mike Almy's expertise in offering unique and quality distilled spirits, seems to be a "golden" match. Undoubtedly, together this dynamic duo will carry the company to obtain its goals as they seek to expand their presence and grow their business.

Colorado Gold Distillery Photo Album

Peter Caciola

Mike Almy

Outside the distillery

Inside the distillery

Bottling whiskey

The final product: Colorado Gold Straight Bourbon Whiskey

Chapter 7
Coulter & Payne Farm Distillery

Shawnee Bend Farms
Union, MO 63084
(636) 395-7418

coulterandpaynefarmdistillery.com
info@coulterandpayne.com

Established
2011

Leadership
Chris Burnette, President, Owner and Head Distiller
Elise Burnette, Vice-President and Owner
William Uphouse, Distiller and Owner
Matt Schimmel, Distiller and Owner

Product Lineup:
Bourbon(s)
Coulter & Payne Bourbon
Coulter & Payne Single Barrel Bourbon

Other
Moonshine, Vodka and Sorghum Rum

"Even with our growth plans, we will remain dedicated to craft production. We will not risk quality by taking a mass production approach."
-Chris Burnette

If Chris Burnette was true to his family roots, at some point, he was going to get into the whiskey business. Where he grew up, almost everyone knows someone who is in the whiskey business. Even if they aren't in it themselves, and most of Chris' family was, they know people who are in the whiskey business!

No, he's not from Kentucky!

Yes, Kentucky is the epicenter of whiskey distilling in the United States. We're talking legitimately being in the whiskey-making business in Kentucky, though. You see, where Chris is from, the Appalachian Mountains of Eastern Tennessee near the Georgia border, there is a whole different kind of whiskey business going on.

That's right, Eastern Tennessee is moonshine country!

To honestly answer any question you may have, yes, Chris Burnette did always know people in the moonshine business. While he was never a "shiner" himself, he had seen it being made and continued enjoyed picking up a bottle when he would go home to visit.

For a while, it didn't seem as though it was going to be the path Chris would follow. After high school he joined the U.S. Air Force and then enrolled in Northern Arizona University after his time in the military. While attending college, studying law, he met Elise, his future wife. They fell in love, got married, and after graduation they moved to Kirkwood, Missouri, where Elise grew up.

Chris became a practicing attorney, specializing in environmental law. Life was good, and being a lawyer, Chris avoided the "family business," other than occasionally imbibing some of that fantastic Eastern Tennessee whiskey. (In his defense, it's tough to cast judgment on a guy when the hometown offering was so much better than anything he could find on store shelves.)

Chris and Elise were moving right along in their lives in Kirkwood when Elise's father passed away leaving she and her brother a small car dealership and a farm in nearby Union, Missouri, about an hour from Kirkwood.

Chris and Elise, along with Elise's brother, knew they didn't want the auto business, but they weren't willing to simply sell off the farm. They began talking about what they could do, and they quickly came up with the idea of Elise's brother living at the property and still keeping it a working farm. The product they would produce, though, would be distilled spirits.

No, Chris wasn't moving the family business up from Eastern Tennessee. We're talking a legitimate farm distillery, self-contained on the old family farm.

Just because he was "going legit" didn't mean he wouldn't call upon his family heritage to incorporate into his new business. He spoke to his grandmother, who detailed the ingredients and the process his family had utilized for generations to make whiskey in the middle of Eastern Tennessee woods of the Appalachian Mountains.

Chris and his brother-in-law began practicing distilling on the back porch of the farm house in 1997. They would experiment and tweak ingredient lists to get just the taste they were looking for. Okay, technically, by the letter of the law, Chris was a moonshiner at this point in the eyes of the U.S. Government. Not only can you not produce distilled spirits to sell, you cannot even produce them for personal consumption.

After several years of getting the farm and personal affairs in order, working on recipes and filling out the necessary paperwork to start a distillery, in 2011 they opened Mad Buffalo Distillery. The company was supplied its organic non-GMO grains from Shawnee Bend Farm, the farm they had started on the land left by Elise's father (according to Missouri law a farm cannot be a distillery so their businesses had to be run as separate entities).

It turns out, it's not just individuals from his hometown who crave real Appalachian-style moonshine because his product began selling very well right away. During each step of the journey, they focused on farm principles to guide them. Because they were growing the grains which would ultimately end up as their product, they got very detailed in starting the process at the earth and seeds level. They harvest the grains and process them right on site, meaning they are one of only about 15 distilleries in the country to actually do this. Chris notes the very nature of what they are doing means the reviews of their product always fall squarely on his family's shoulders. After all, from seed to bottle, and everything in between, is controlled by them.

The bourbon they produce follows suit with this concept. In order for a smoother bourbon they are removing 5% – 10% of their product right away so only the best of what they produce goes into the barrels. They then age their bourbon for 6 – 7 months in 15 gallon barrels. While it isn't science, master distillers for the big distilleries have said this is about the equivalent of 18 months of aging in 53 gallon barrels.

Chris is almost fanatical in his dedication to producing a locally made product. Not only is everything in the bottle locally made, so are the barrels he is aging it in (from nearby Cuba, Missouri), the bottles are made by a company which uses sand from Pacific, Missouri (15 minutes away) and the labels are printed in St. Louis. Literally the only thing not locally produced for Chris' products is the bottle caps. He cannot find a producer in Missouri for those so he begrudgingly uses a vendor in Minnesota.

The end result for his bourbon is a smooth tasting, uniquely local product.

Starting any business has its hiccups, and Chris and his family recognized they had made a mistake in calling their company Mad Buffalo Distillery. The name didn't capitalize on their greatest asset, the fact they are truly a farm distillery. There is so much to offer from the fact they grow the grain used in their product, to the fact all of their grains are grown without using chemicals to simple notions like they don't waste anything at the farm (spent mash is given to surrounding farms for use by their livestock, for instance). They knew they were missing out on a real opportunity to convey this message with their name.

Unfortunately, the company was growing quickly which compounded the issues of changing the name, so what to do? Keep what you are doing based on some moderate success or totally rebrand yourself to capture the essence of what you are truly doing?

For Chris and his family, they knew they were in it for the long haul and while this may cause them some short-term growing pains, they elected to rebrand themselves to reflect who they truly were. In 2014, they became Coulter & Payne Farm Distillery using family names from both Elise's family and Chris'.

Today, they are producing their aged products under the Coulter and Payne name and their unaged offerings under the name Crop Circle Spirits (a fun name, yet still with an underlying farming theme). The rebranding is already paying dividends as consumers seem to automatically understand the notion of a small, local offering of the products being released under the Coulter and Payne Farm Distillery brand versus the more generic sounding Mad Buffalo name.

The farm has one limitation in that it doesn't allow visitors. They simply aren't set-up to be enable droves of people coming through a residential area to pay them a visit. This just means they work harder to get out in the community, sponsoring events and tastings to get their name out there. Long-term, a second piece of property could house a farm store where they would bring products from Shawnee Bend Farm directly to consumers, and they do envision also putting a Coulter and Payne tasting room there.

For Chris and his family it's been a tremendous experience building something not only his family owns, but their employees do as well. Chris, his wife and brother-in-law all recognized the value of not only having employees but employees who were truly vested in what they were doing. Not vested in a story or message, truly stakeholders in the company. With this in mind, they set their company up as an employee-owned organization with workers getting stock which grows in value by increasing shares every year.

This means the future of the company is already determined. It will be a company wholly-owned by its employees (the shares of the family members who started the company slowly decrease over time as employees' share grow ensuring a smooth transition of ownership well beyond the family).

Not only is the future leadership set, so is the vision of the company. The plan is to grow as big as the market will bear. They certainly would like to be in all 50 states, and the idea of exporting product overseas sounds like something they would like to do as well. Despite the lofty ideas of continuing to expand outward from Missouri, the Coulter & Payne team is dedicated to keeping their production approach exactly as it is now. This means no matter how big they get, production will be limited to 500 gallon mash starters. It's almost crazy to think about when you consider the largest producers of distilled spirits are beginning with mash blends exceeding 100,000 gallons to meet demand but Chris and team plan to stay with a small batch approach to maintain quality and consistency. If this means expanding production for more mash tanks and stills and running around-the-clock, so be it. Coulter & Payne Farm Distillery is a small batch distiller!

With this dedication, it sounds like the farm is going to be a pretty busy place. Whether you are in Fairbanks, Alaska, Kilauea, Hawaii, Bangor, Maine or San Diego, California, get ready… Coulter & Payne should be heading your way soon!

Coulter & Payne Farm Distillery Photo Album

Chris & Elise Burnette

Inspecting the still

Coulter & Payne is located on a working farm

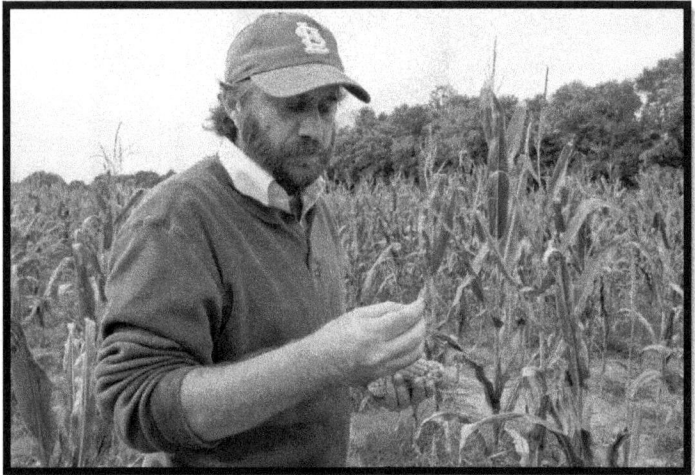

This means the raw ingredients are gathered just steps from where they distill their products

The base for Coulter & Payne's bourbon is an old family recipe passed down through generations of Chris' family

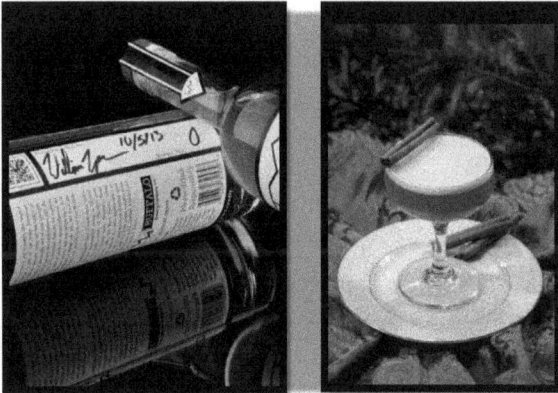

Coulter & Payne Farm Distillery's bourbon is equally enjoyable neat as it is in a cocktail

Chapter 8
Dark Corner Distillery

241-B North Main Street
Greensville, SC 29601
(864) 631-1144

darkcornerdistillery.com
info@darkcornerdistillery.com

Established
2011

Leadership
Joe Fenten, Founder & President

Product Lineup:
Bourbon(s)
Lewis Redmond Carolina Bourbon Whiskey

Other
Corn Whiskey (Apple & Peach) & Whiskey

"Where I grew up, you could smell the moonshine being made in the woods behind a nearby peach orchard."
   -Joe Fenten

Despite no credible evidence Bigfoot actually exists, the debate continues to draw interest as to whether or not ape-like animals live in remote areas, avoiding all human contact other than the occasional out-of-focus camera.

There are people who will tell you Yale's Skull and Bones secret society actually pulls the strings on almost every major economic decision in the United States.

Supposedly, a UFO crashed near Roswell, New Mexico, in 1947. People still flock there today, over 60 years later, to see what it's all about.

The bottom line is people love mystery and intrigue. The "Dark Corner" of South Carolina garners this sort of fascination for people. Native son Joe Fenten, not only knows how curious people are about the area, he's benefitted from being part of this mysterious place as he started the business he named after it.

Joe grew up near Greenville, South Carolina, in the area known as the "Dark Corner." This term dates back to the unrest before the Civil War as legendary political leader John C. Calhoun was trying to lead a movement for the State of South Carolina to nullify federal law. When constituents near Greenville voted against his plan, the two-time Vice-President of the United States (under John Q. Adams and Andrew Jackson), was angrily quoted as stating, "The light will never again shine on that dark corner of the state." The area gained a reputation as being mysterious since no one was willing to own up to being part of Calhoun's "dark corner" so visitors were always told the dark corner was "a little further up the road." When they would proceed to the town" a little further up the road," it would only yield the exact same response: "The 'Dark Corner' was yet still further up the road." Before long, a trip further up the road meant you were in North Carolina, which is exactly where the residents wanted those unwelcome visitors.

While interest in political dissent may have dissipated over the years, the mystery surrounding the Dark Corner remained as it would eventually become a hotbed for another illicit activity: moonshining. This "whispered-about" reputation as being the place to get the best 'shine, led to unwelcome visitors trying to get their hands on some Dark Corner hooch. Unfortunately for them, the code for strangers was adhered to by the locals, and they were given the same "further up the road" plan which had been utilized in the past.

Hello, Asheville, North Carolina!

While attending Clemson, studying engineering, Joe Fenten got into the distilled spirits business. No, he wasn't working a still out in the woods under the cover of darkness; he was a bartender, mixing drinks.

After graduating, he went to work as an electrical engineer. As a contractor, he worked across the United States. Most of the jobs he was working were at nuclear power plants. He always knew there was something more for him. Yet, he just wasn't sure what it was going to be. Distilled spirits were probably the furthest thing from his mind.

You see, Joe Fenten, the former bartender, and a guy who grew up in the moonshining capital of South Carolina, wasn't much of a drinker. In fact, he hadn't even tried a beer. Not that he had anything against consuming beer. It's just something he kind of never got around to doing.

Joe's interest in the distilled spirits industry would come via a unique assignment he got on his job. It was what he thought would be a nice diversion from the power plants. The game changer came when he was given a job at a distillery which was looking to increase production. During Joe's two+ months working at the distillery, many of which were 16 hour days, Joe got to know the staff and learn about the business.

His interest was piqued with the process of making alcohol, the science behind it, and, most importantly, the profit margins. It didn't take a whole lot of calculations to figure out this was a business worth looking into.

Joe went to work on a business plan. With the precision his engineering background afforded him, he carefully plotted out every detail. His approach was extremely helpful in streamlining what is typically a very arduous process in the paperwork and the filings necessary to start a distilled spirits company.

From start-to-finish, Joe's tactical approach of systematically checking off the list of everything he needed to do to start his distillery took 364 days. On June 23, 2011, Joe received his federal permit, allowing him to open his distillery. He celebrated his accomplishment by drinking a beer. Yes, it's true, the first time he tried a beer was the day he got the licensing needed to open a company which produces alcohol.

The name for his new endeavor was obvious. Dark Corner sounds equally as mysterious whether or not you know the history but is incredibly important to those in the area around

Greenville. Joe was building a company which would highlight the best of the area, and it seemed like a natural fit to name his business after the place where he grew up and gave so much to him.

Of course, once that first beer got cracked, Joe had to go to work. This meant he needed to get up-to-speed on the flavor profiles so he could begin to formulate his own recipes. Luckily, as a person who grew up in the Dark Corner, Joe wasn't given the "further up the road" treatment typically dished out by the locals. Soon, mason jars full of samples from the woods of the Dark Corner began showing up whereby Joe would compare-and-contrast them to the national brands.

Perhaps it was the outsider's view of someone who didn't drink a lot of distilled spirits before which allowed Joe to go in without any preconceived notions and draw the best from everything he tried. Admittedly, at first, making whiskey was a struggle. Joe likens his first attempt at distilling as yielding a raw whiskey which tasted like rotten pineapple and cottage cheese. Undeterred, Joe learned from the mistakes and vowed to increase quality and taste with his next test batch. It was this engineering approach which yielded Joe's plan of:

get samples ˃ taste ˃ formulate ˃ create ˃ taste ˃ refine ˃

reformulate ˃ recreate ˃ repeat.

Dark Corner Distillery's Lewis Redmond Carolina Bourbon Whiskey is named after a local folk hero. From 1870 – 1884, Major Lewis Redmond avoided capture from federal authorities as the leading producer of moonshine in the area. Locals loved the fact he was able to skirt authorities despite his high profile status with the feds who wanted to shut down his illegal operation. His legend only grew when he was finally arrested in 1884. U.S. President Chester A. Arthur granted him a full pardon in exchange for simply taking his whiskey making business legit.

Joe Fenten uses the white whiskey (a.k.a. moonshine) he was able to perfect through all of his sampling, testing and reformulations as the base for his Lewis Redmond Bourbon. In blind taste tests, Dark Corner is consistently beating out the nationally-known competitors with its moonshine, so it's clearly a great start to creating an outstanding bourbon. It's a mash of corn, red wheat and barley. Joe ages it in barrels ranging from 5 – 30 gallons right in view in his 100 year-old restored building in downtown Greenville. The yield is a soft oak-tasting bourbon with flavor notes of vanilla and caramel.

For Joe, the highlight of what he is doing is the continued process of learning and perfecting his product in the distilled spirits business. The process is never complete. He continues to refine and evolve to make his next batch better than the last.

Joe is in the process of building a new facility which will significantly increase his capacity. Dark Corner is continually adding new markets, and there seems to be no ceiling as to how big the company can get.

When asked, Joe shrugs off any inquiries about where he expects his company to be in five years, stating he's just going where it takes him. He sees opportunities from market expansion as well as some contraction of competitors who have entered the market based on the novelty of joining the suddenly hot and trendy world of distilled spirits.

Even with only the base knowledge of a single interview, it's obvious Joe isn't a "fly by the seat of your pants without a plan kinda guy." When challenged, he concedes he's thought through where he wants to be in five years and how he will get there. Those plans will remain his, though.

For the rest of us… well, we just get to enjoy the fruits of his labor with his unique take on creating some outstanding whiskies!

Dark Corner Distillery Photo Album

Joe Fenten

Inside Dark Corner Distillery

Cooking time

Aging time

Filling moonshine by hand

Dark Corner Distillery product lineup

Chapter 9
Grand Traverse Distillery

781 Industrial Circle Drive, Suite 5
Traverse City, MI 49686
(231) 947-8635

grandtraversedistillery.com
info@grandtraversedistillery.com

Established
2005

Leadership
Kent Rabish, Owner

Product Lineup:
Bourbon(s)
Grand Traverse Distillery 100% Straight Bourbon Whiskey

Other
Vodka, Rum, Gin & Whiskey

"Because of our size, we can get our customers involved in some of the experiments we do. It's okay for us to do four barrels runs of unique products like the Peated Malted Barley & Rye Whiskey we will have coming out soon."
      -Kent Rabish

As the craft distilling revolution has grown, consumers have become increasing aware of, and interested in, seeking out local products. There probably isn't a segment within craft distilling where "buying local" is more important than it is with bourbon. While many factors go into making a great bourbon, one of the most important is the aging process. Aging bourbon is more than liquid sitting in a barrel. It's an interaction which ebbs and flows with seasonal changes. Depending on the time of the year, the bourbon-in-the-making is going to expand into or contract back out of the barrel based on the weather and conditions outside of the barrel.

For the true bourbon fan, it becomes a quest to sample bourbons from different regions in the United States to taste the impact climate and individual distilleries processes have on their whiskey. There certainly are many other factors which are going to impact the taste of a bourbon, starting with the raw ingredients. Other areas to consider include the location of the barrels (are they stored inside or outside?), the size of the barrels, the time inside the barrels and even the weather patterns during the time the product is aging. Despite the fact of never achieving a true apples-to-apples type of comparison, at its most basic, the most fervent bourbon connoisseurs want to compare the taste of a Kentucky bourbon versus a Michigan distilled offering versus one made in Colorado and so on.

The very nature of picking up a **Special Bourbon Edition** of a book likely means you fall into the of world bourbon fandom. You're probably shaking your head in agreement regarding the quest of seeking out local in search of the best bourbon money can buy.

Not everyone is like you, though.

In the distilled spirits world, bourbon is clearly *the* thing right now. It hasn't been this hot since it was "the only thing" back in the old gunslinger days. The rapid boost in popularity for "America's Distilled Spirit" means our corn-based aged whiskey has a bevy of new fans. Consumers, so new to trying to find an undiscovered gem are often buying the latest offerings and coolest-looking labels.

What these bourbon-newbies may be missing is one small word: *distilled*. Often they are seeing a package with a name which sounds uniquely local, and the labeling plays up the company's "local" roots. Again, what's missing is the word distilled. In place of it are words like "packaged by" or "bottled by."

As soon as you replace "distilled by" with "bottled by" or any other close-sounding, yet totally different meaning words, you have a product which likely isn't local at all. In fact, you can almost guarantee it was either made in Kentucky by one of the large distilleries, selling off excess stock, or a large provider in Indiana which specializes in providing outsourced bourbon and other distilled spirits for those wanting to label them as their company's product.

Let's be perfectly clear. There isn't anything inherently wrong, immoral or illegal about any of this. In fact, there are plenty of reasons why a company would do this... not the least of which is the amount of time it takes to age bourbon means it's an incredibly expensive and slow process to get into the business. It's simply easier to buy it premade from someone else.

The more a company tries to mask the fact they have bought their product, and not actually made it begins to cloud what is morally the right approach for consumers. After all, isn't a company which relies on product completely outsourced to a manufacturer simply a marketing company and not a distiller?

No matter where you personally stand on this issue, the truth is, there certainly isn't an experience of "buying local" in the world of bourbon if your "local" company is just slapping a label on product distilled in Kentucky or Indiana.

Kent Rabish of Grand Traverse Distillery has made it a personal quest to educate consumers regarding truly buying a local product. Not just a label saying it was "bottled" locally, either. Kent is speaking of truly local in that he is starting with local ingredients, distilling and bottling it onsite at his company's hometown of Traverse City, Michigan.

The reason Kent is so adamant about focusing his business on this fact is it's truly how he got into owning his distillery. After graduating with biology and chemistry degrees, Kent went to work in pharmaceutical sales. He enjoyed the work and really wasn't looking to do anything else. On a vacation to Oregon in 2001, Kent went to a craft distillery and ordered a flight, which contained two vodkas, two gins and a cordial. This was just a tourist visit. Kent, a confirmed vodka fan, enjoyed the big name imported vodkas and really had low expectations for these offerings being produced in Bend, Oregon.

As he tried the vodkas, he simply couldn't believe the quality of the product he was sampling. These vodkas rivaled the high-end imports he enjoyed and had previously professed his loyalty. He immediately started thinking about getting into the business.

After returning to Michigan, his first step was to research the idea. He anticipated roadblocks, so he would take the approach of delving in by asking questions of himself and his quest:

Why can't we open a distillery?

Why wouldn't we open a distillery?

What's stopping us?

Because he was so early in the craft distilling industry, it literally took him 3 – 4 years of research to get going. His final step was attending the American Distillers Institute's convention in Alameda, California. The organization was just getting going, and there were only about 50 attendees. Still, he managed to meet some suppliers and other people already in the business who were extremely helpful and encouraging.

In 2005, Grand Traverse Distillery was officially opened. Though there aren't official records, Kent's glass supplier told him at the time he was like the 30th distillery in the country. When you compare that to 700 in 2014, up from 500 in 2013, you see how quickly the numbers could easily top out in the 1,000 – 1,200 range in 2015. Reviewing these eye-popping stats, you begin to get a feel for how quickly the industry has sprung up.

Prior to owning the business, Kent had very limited distilling experience. As a student of biology and chemistry, he did have an interest in the science of distillation back in college and ran some experiments with distilling wine (he was a college student so this may be more appropriately written as "experiments"). That was the limit of his personal experience.

In addition to the advice Kent got through the connections he made at the American Distilling Institute, his representative from Arnold Holstein, the distillery manufacturer in southern Germany, has also been an incredible resource. Not only did he work with Kent with the build out, his rep stayed onsite for several days afterward training him to use the equipment. Plus, the support continued long after he left as Kent would continue to call upon him every time he started making a new type of distilled spirit.

Grand Traverse Distillery's 100% Straight Bourbon contains a mash of 70% corn, 20% rye and 10% malted barley. It's aged for 3 years, and Kent points out he takes deep cuts to ensure it's as smooth as it can be starting out in the barrel.

After sitting in the barrels for three years, the final product has a unique taste you can only find in a bourbon manufactured in Traverse City, Michigan!

One thing Kent loves about being a craft distiller is the fact you aren't beholden to the distribution model the big guys have to live with. He literally can experiment and bring his offerings directly to consumers. He is getting very close to one unique whiskey he is calling Islay Rye. It's a peated malted barley and rye whiskey. The earthy taste of the peated malted barley is a unique balance to the clean and crisp taste of the rye. Kent's customers can have a unique whiskey experience which would likely never be offered through one of the companies which serve as the industry standards in bourbon. Their model would force them to create thousands and thousands of barrels which is truly going to be a niche market for individuals seeking something unique. Kent, on the other hand, can offer this a four-barrel run and expand upon that if it finds an audience.

Kent's model for growth is a tactical approach, very different than typically found in the craft distilling world. He's opening up tasting rooms in areas known for tourism. Currently, he has three in addition to the one attached to his distillery. Those others are in Frankenmuth, Leland and Grand Rapids. He's also partnered with Black Star Farms Winery to split two additional tasting rooms in Northwest Michigan. These two additional sites offer both Black Star Farms' wines and Grand Traverse Distillery's distilled spirits.

Kent's approach is working. He recently hired a second distiller which will double production. He continues to focus on whiskey as being the means of future growth for his company. Even with concerns of the market becoming saturated with so many distilleries and consumers' tastes shifting while all of these distilleries have whiskey aging in barrels, Kent's not worried.

He knows it doesn't matter if the market would shrink a bit; there's always going to be the need for quality whiskey with a unique profile, and he's got some great whiskey. All **distilled** and bottled in Traverse City, Michigan (check his label... it says it right there).

Grand Traverse Distillery Photo Album

Kent Rabish

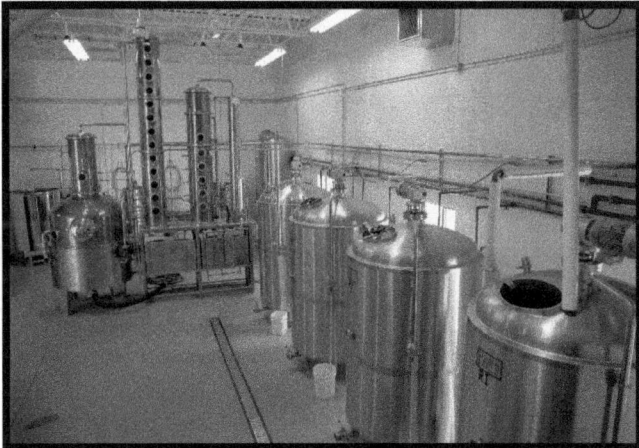

Grand Traverse Distillery's production area

Send Brothers' Farm in Williamsburg, Michigan where Grand Traverse Distillery purchase 100% of its wheat, corn and rye

Kent at the still

Filling bottles

I will take a Grand Traverse Distillery 100% Straight Bourbon Whiskey… neat, please!

Chapter 10
Heritage Distilling Co.

HERITAGE®
D I S T I L L I N G C°
3207 57th Street Court NW
Gig Harbor, WA 98335
(253) 509-0008

heritagedistilling.com
info@heritagedistilling.com

Established
2011

Leadership
Jennifer Stiefel, Founder and President and Justin Stiefel, Founder, CEO & Master Distiller

Product Lineup:
Bourbon(s)
Elk Rider Bourbon

Other
Vodka, Gin, Whiskey and customized spirits through Heritage Distilling's Cask Club® and My Batch® programs

"The artistry in whiskey making lies in patience."
-Justin Stiefel

It's rare to have an extended conversation with an owner of a distillery where, at some point, the discussion doesn't turn to legislation and the local, state and federal laws governing the distilled spirits industry. All of the laws and regulations governing the industry means anyone involved literally becomes a walking encyclopedia of alcohol-related rules and regulations. Additionally, as the federal laws began to loosen up over the last 15 – 20 years, many of the individuals in the business have been personally involved in working with local and state lawmakers in crafting the laws pertaining to craft distilling in the communities where they are doing business.

Having spent eight years working in the United States Senate, Heritage Distilling co-founder and master distiller Justin Stiefel doesn't just know distilled spirits legislation. With a chemical engineering degree as well as a law degree, he secured work in a Washington, D.C. law firm. He worked eight years in the Senate, as Council, Chief of Staff and Press Secretary for a senator from Alaska. In his time in the U.S. Senate, he was involved in crafting legislation pertaining to a variety of issues; even going through the arduous process of drafting legislature from scratch.

Justin grew up in Spokane, Washington. He got his first figurative taste of distilling in the seventh grade. For a science project in a chemistry lab, he made his first batch of distillation. You don't have to own a deep understanding of alcohol legislation to realize today you probably couldn't get away with introducing seventh graders to distilling spirits by making alcohol in seventh grade chemistry!

Despite the early interest and introduction to creating alcohol, it didn't look like it would be a career path for Justin. He was a hobby brewer and wine maker in college, but his studies for chemical engineering and law school kept him pretty busy.

By the time he graduated, it seemed as though his brewing and wine making days were behind him. He had married Jennifer, his high school sweetheart, and they both had great jobs in Washington, D.C. After eight years in the nation's capital both Jennifer and Justin began to yearn for their home state of Washington. All of their family still remained in the area. The weather was better. Their history and heritage remained in the Pacific Northwest.

Plus, eight years working in the political system is a grind. It's stressful with long hours and a fast pace. As Justin and Jennifer compared and contrasted staying in D.C. versus returning home to Washington, they realized everything they needed was back in their home in the state of Washington. Their minds were made up; they simply needed a game plan to get home.

Being keenly aware of laws and regulations, Justin knew the laws had begun to loosen up in the State of Washington in regards to distilling. With his chemical engineering background and experience as a hobby brewer/wine maker, he and Jennifer found the idea of opening their own business very appealing. There were several reasons they decided to focus on distilled spirits instead of beer or wine. Justin felt distilled spirits was an easier path than beer or wine. While rudimentary in the equipment needs compared to distilled spirits, beer and wine have a much higher chance of making mistakes and ruining batches. There aren't errors in the world of distilled spirits. If your product doesn't taste exactly as you envision when you were crafting it, you simply run it through the still again. It just seemed to be a much more forgiving medium to the Stiefels.

The other, and perhaps more pressing reason behind their decision, was the fact both craft beer and wine making had already taken off in the Pacific Northwest. The area was not only at the forefront of the microbrewery/brewpub revolution, the State of Washington was home to more than 800 wineries.

With their path now set on distilling, Jennifer and Justin began working on a name for their company. They quickly took to the name Heritage Distilling. They liked the fact the word "heritage" conveys a nod to the past and remembering traditions. The company itself was not only bringing Justin and Jennifer back to their roots, it would become part of their story... their own "personal heritage." They couldn't fall in love with the name, though, as they were sure it already have been claimed by someone. Almost unbelievably, it was available, so the Stiefels secured it and officially had a name for their company.

Their Elk Rider Bourbon draws upon the concept of heritage for the Stiefels. Jennifer's family were some of the early pioneers as Americans began to head to the Pacific Northwest. In the late 1800s, with a family of 17, they were amongst the first homesteaders in the Olympic Range. Undoubtedly, one of the most unique components of Jennifer's family's heritage was the fact her ancestors actually tamed and domesticated elk. They became famous by making appearances at events riding the majestic beasts. One of their most well-known events was appearing at the yearly Parade of Roses in Portland. There are some great old photographs of her family members, all women in full-length dresses, riding elk in formation.

Their bourbon is a high rye bourbon with strong pepper notes. Justin slow blends the infusion of water to maintain his flavor profile. He never goes below 92 proof which many other distillers do resulting in much of the character and flavor being stripped out. The end result is a creamier and more viscous tasting experience for their Elk Rider Bourbon.

While Justin handles the distilling duties, Jennifer's arena is Heritage Distilling's customer experience. She has gotten very creative in offering some unique ways to connect with customers. First of all, the company's tasting room is a sensory experience. In addition to being able to touch, view and taste all of the company's products, the production area is a floor below the tasting room. Guests not only get to see the team working, they get to smell everything.

A true experience appealing to all senses!

Secondly, Heritage Distilling connects with its customers through two unique programs. With their Cask Club®, guests get a 10 liter mini barrel, or cask with the type of spirit selected by the customer. The customer then decides how long their bourbon, rye, single malt whiskey, vodka or gin is in the cask. They can pull out a bottle with a custom designed label at any time and enjoy it at barrel strength or infuse water to pull the proof down. The barrels even are personalized by the customer and adorn the tasting room, adding to the overall ambiance.

Another program they offer is called My Batch®, and it also appeals to customers looking to have more say in their distilled spirits. With this offering, the customer takes a distilling course at Heritage's facility. They then make their own distilled spirits in one of the company's six mini-stills. They get the opportunity to buy bottles of the final product and can even get a two liter mini-cask to age the creation at their home.

The Heritage team is proud of these programs as they put the taste of their final product into the hands of the customer. Most of the distilled spirits on the market today are produced by large multinational companies and their master distillers are controlling how their brands taste. This means there are relatively few people determining how most distilled spirits like bourbon taste. When you consider the market share of these big brands, you quickly realize these few individuals are controlling the drinking experiences for most of the population.

The Heritage Distilling Co. approach is you decide how your spirits should taste, not a megabrand product manager.

Jennifer and Justin are pleased with the idea that not only do their customers enjoy their products, they are good stewards of their community. They look to continue growing their brand while retaining their identity as a local company. Their ultimate goal is to create a brand that is local no matter where you are buying it.

Jennifer and Justin don't just have a brand with Heritage Distilling… they have their past, present and future!

Heritage Distilling Co. Photo Album

Justin & Jennifer Stiefel

Bottling rye whiskey

The mini-stills used in Heritage Distilling Co.'s My Batch®
program

The full size version

Casks in the Tasting Room at Heritage Distilling Co.

Detailed look at a Cask Club® member's cask

Blood orange is one of their flavored vodka offerings

Heritage Distilling Co. product lineup

Chapter 11
Journeyman Distillery

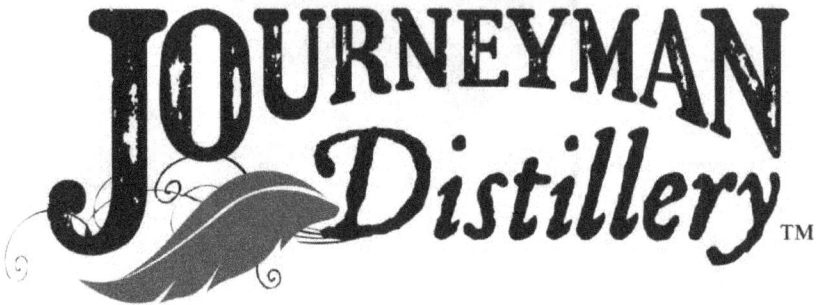

JOURNEYMAN Distillery™

109 Generations Drive
Three Oaks, MI 49128
(269) 820-2050

journeymandistillery.com
info@journeymandistillery.com

Established
2009

Leadership
Bill Welter, Founder

Product Lineup:
Bourbon(s)
Featherbone Bourbon Whiskey

Other
Gin, Rye, Vodka, Whiskey, Jalapeno Spirit, Coffee Liqueur, Moonshine, Single Malt Whiskey & Rum

"The most satisfying aspect of the business is seeing our customers enjoying our product as much as we enjoy making it."
-Daniel Milsk, Journeyman Distillery

For over 30 years, the Welter family business was a bank founded by Bill Welter's father in Valparaiso, Indiana. When the bank was sold, Bill wasn't exactly sure what he would do moving forward.

As he explored his options, he decided to take a working sabbatical in Scotland, where the former Division I golfer could play some of the finest courses in the world. While living in Scotland, not only did Bill hone his golf game, but also several occurrences came together to help define his future.

First, he worked at a restaurant where he learned the behind the scenes details of running a company in the food and beverage industry. Second, he gained an affinity for fine local whiskies available as well as an appreciation for how they were made. Finally, he befriended Greg Ramsay, owner of New Zealand Whisky Co. who was in Scotland on vacation. As Bill prepared to move back to the United States, he put these three components together to formulate his plans for the future.

The passion he had developed for both distilling and fine whiskey, combined with the hands-on work he had done at the restaurant, gave him the base of knowledge to run his own distillery. The friendship of Greg Ramsay gave him a sounding board from someone who was already successful in the business and could assist him with the artistry of creating the same type of distilled spirits he had found in Europe.

Initially, Bill looked into opening his business back home in Valparaiso. As he looked a little deeper, he found the local and state laws to be too prohibitive to run the company in the manner he envisioned.

In researching the laws of states in the area, Bill found Michigan's to be the most inviting, so he turned his focus to starting his business there. With no personal ties or connection to the State of Michigan, Bill wasn't locked into any city or part of the state. He was simply determined to open up the company where the situation felt right.

To determine where to open his distillery, he took his search on the road. He just got into his car and drove city-to-city in Michigan. He checked out the lay of the land and the buzz of the heart of the downtowns. Were there any suitable locations to open a business for him? In reality, he didn't know exactly what he was looking for; he just knew he'd know what he wanted when he found it.

Bill's quest culminated with a visit to Three Oaks, Michigan. There, he found an abandoned factory which had once housed the Warren Featherbone Company.

The Warren Featherbone Company was named after Edward Kirk "E.K." Warren, its founder. The plant produced corsets using the quills of feathers instead of the traditional whale bone which had always been the standard. The result of using the "featherbone" was a higher quality product which didn't get brittle over time and was also cheaper. Soon, E.K. Warren's creation became the new industry standard for women's corsets, and he became a very wealthy man, owning large plots of land which would eventually be donated to the State of Michigan, creating parks which are still in use today.

Finding a location to domicile his company was the first step for Bill in starting his business. He now had to come up with a name for his new venture. Unlike finding a location, the idea for the name came quickly for him. His new business would be called Journeyman Distillery as a nod to his personal journey to get his company going. His own journey, taking him from his hometown of Valparaiso to Scotland and all over Michigan without a clear starting or stopping point meant the name Journeyman Distillery perfectly captured the spirit of his life in forming the company.

Even with the name established, Bill still had a long road ahead. The factory he had discovered closed in the 1950s, and it wasn't much more than a shell. Bill saw the potential of utilizing the factory as much more than a place for production. The town of Three Oaks is a popular tourist destination for Chicago residents, and he really wanted to make his factory a place where visitors would not only feel welcome the first time they came by but it would be a place they would like to visit time-after-time.

A look around today confirms Bill Welter has been able to achieve his goal. The new building retains the "old factory" feel while still being modern and inviting. In addition to production and touring facilities and a tasting room, Journeyman Distillery has 2,000 square feet of meeting space for large events.

Drawing upon his work in the restaurant business in Scotland, Bill has even taken his business beyond simply a distillery. He has a chef on staff, who offers a unique culinary experience for visitors, plus their product catalog includes food offerings such as chocolates, Luxardo Cherries and Barrel Aged Maple Syrup.

Journeyman's Featherbone Bourbon Whiskey is made up of 70% corn and a combination of wheat and rye to round out the mash. They age their bourbon in both 15 and 30 gallon barrels.

What truly makes Journeyman's bourbon different than its competitors is something which makes all of their offerings unique: it is both organic certified and kosher certified. This means all of the ingredients in the company's products have received both certifications.

The uniqueness of this distinction is realized after doing a little research. While there isn't necessarily a central database to provide a definitive answer, there are only a dozen or so organic distilleries in the United State. Combine that fact with Journeyman's kosher certification as well, you realize they may be in a class by themselves.

Looking at the future you realize Bill Welter's journey has only just begun. Currently, his company's products are available for sale in 13 states and they are at maximum capacity. They are currently under construction to increase the size of their production area by two times. Additional equipment being purchased will increase their capacity by five times.

It makes you wonder what E.K. Warren, the proprietor of the old Warren Featherbone Company who built the factory where Journeyman now operates, would think of all of this. Well, the answer is it would probably be a mixed review. Clearly, Mr. Warren would have to appreciate the fact his factory has been brought back to life thanks to the vision of

Bill Welter. Then again, Mr. Warren may take pause when he realizes it's a distilled spirits company now operating at the old corset factory. You see, Mr. Warren was a staunch prohibitionist well before the Prohibition era even began in the United States.

Despite his stance against the alcohol industry in the early 1900s, it's easy to imagine Mr. Warren coming around when he saw what Bill Welter has been doing in Mr. Warren's old factory.

After all, everyone loves the story of an exciting journey!

Journeyman Distillery Photo Album

Bill Welter at St. Andrews Old Course in Scotland

The pot still nicknamed Willy Wonka at Journeyman

Inside the old Featherbone factory before construction

Inside Journeyman after construction

Make your own: Journeyman's whiskey aging kit

Bill hand-dipping bottles

The bar in the tasting room

Journeyman Distiller Featherbone Bourbon Whiskey

Chapter 12
Mississippi River Distilling Company

MISSISSIPPI RIVER
DISTILLING COMPANY
— Le Claire, Iowa —
303 N. Cody Road
LeClaire, IA 52753
(563) 484-4342

mrdistilling.com
info@mrdistilling.com

Established
2010

Leadership
Ryan and Garrett Burchett, Co-Owners

Product Lineup:
Bourbon(s)
Cody Road Eight Barrel Blend & Cody Road Single Barrel

Other
Vodka, Gin, Artisan Spirit, Rye, Whiskey, Cream Liqueur and
Limited Edition Releases

"Whiskey is the future."
-Ryan Burchett

Growing up, from junior high forward, Ryan and Garrett Burchett worked in the family business. Unfortunately for them, the family business was road construction. The days were hot, the hours were long and the work was hard. It's the kind of work where you dream of going into the office one day, tell the boss to go to hell and start your own business.

That doesn't happen when you dad is your boss, though. The one thing the family business taught the Burchett boys was that you don't want to go into the family business. Go to school, study hard, apply yourself and land a good job. The kind of work where you never have to think, "I'm quitting this gig and starting my own company."

The plan worked for the Burchett boys... almost. They did go to college and managed to land some great jobs. The kind of work anyone would envy. Ryan was a chief meteorologist on an NBC affiliate in Davenport, Iowa. Garrett was a transportation engineer working in Dallas.

Still, despite the prestigious jobs, something was missing. Garrett realized working in traffic management as a transportation engineer meant it would be unlikely he would ever be able to get home to Iowa. Typically, only very large urban cities employ transportation engineers.

Ryan loved his job, but he had moved multiple times and continued career growth would have likely meant more moves. Plus, he was now married and had a child and found himself missing family events with the hours associated with the job. When a storm rolled in, the hours would grow even longer.

Both brothers had begun to feel the itch to make a change about the time the laws in Iowa modified to encourage craft distillers to open up shop there. Garrett was first to broach the subject. When a news story came out highlighting the fact distilleries could offer customers the chance to taste or buy their product on premise, he joked Ryan and he should get into the business.

It remained a pipe dream between the brothers for a brief time: a conversation in which they would both get out of the restrictions of their current jobs, return to their hometown and be able to work together.

Before you know it, they began to get semi-serious, putting together a business plan. The ideas seemed to flow easily for the pair. They wanted a distillery which showcased the products from the local farmers. They even planned to offer an education about Iowa corn to visitors by milling it at their facility. Not only did this allow visitors to see real Iowa corn being used in their distilled spirits, it made perfect financial sense. A bushel of milled corn cost approximately $50. They could buy the same amount of corn to make that bushel onsite for $8 - $10.

This was to be a facility in which every aspect appealed to the tourism industry. The show *American Pickers* is filmed there, and the store they run, Antique Archaeology, brings lots of tourists to the area with few other attractions to enjoy. Plus, their planned location would be right on the Mississippi River, a classic symbol of not only LeClaire, Iowa, but America itself.

Their education about creating distilled spirts came from an unusual source: their still vendor. While they were doing their research, they found a German company making top-of-the-line stills, which was just entering the U.S. market. The support they offered went far beyond just selling them a product. They sponsored training for the pair in both Chicago and Germany. Once they completed the program put together by the still company, they were in business. Plus, their relationship led them to getting a still which would be centerpiece of any distillery. Fashioned out of stainless steel and copper, the still is nicknamed "The Rose." It's a beauty with the curves of a woman and functionality of a workhorse.

Their bourbon is called Cody Road Bourbon named after both the actual road the distillery sits on as well as Buffalo Bill Cody, the hero from the Old West the road was named after. (Buffalo Bill was born about one mile down the road from where Mississippi River Distilling sits today.)

There are several components which make their bourbon offering unique. First of all, it is 20% wheat, meaning it's a wheated bourbon. It's a little sweeter than most bourbons or ryes.

Secondly, the Burchett brothers use barrels about half the size of the standard bourbon aging barrels. This means there is more surface to whiskey interaction, allowing the bourbon to draw more flavor from the barrel as it ages. This gives each barrel a distinct and unique flavor which appeals to Ryan and Garrett who want a product highlighting the fruitiness of the wheat and the sweetness of the corn. They find the offerings from Kentucky to be so smoothed out, the taste is almost uniform no matter what distiller you buy bourbon from.

Finally, the Burchett brothers only add about 5% water to their raw product out of the barrel. When you compare it to the 10% – 20% added by their competitors, you see why the bold taste comes through.

All of the above combined with the hands-on artistry of a crafted bourbon makes for a product consumers seem to be craving. The brothers write the batch and bottle number on the label so consumers can go online and see production notes from each step of the journey from raw ingredients to production, barreling and finally bottling.

The brothers' time outside of the industry has also served them well. They have brought some unique ideas which have created some additional revenue streams. One of their most popular ideas is Whiskey School. Once a year they spend a weekend at the distillery with 10 enthusiastic students who want to learn everything there is to know about whiskey. They review raw ingredients, prepare a batch, cook a mash, barrel product and even bottle it. Time between lessons is spent tasting product and enjoying meals cooked with their Mississippi River Distilling products.

They also offer a program they have entitled My Whiskey in which individuals can put together their own recipe, get involved in the production of the product and then buy the entire barrel. Final cost of the approximate 150 bottles yielded is right in line with any craft bourbon, and the customer gets the satisfaction of presenting a whiskey they made to friends and family.

Business is going great for the Burchett brothers. They feel after four years they have made it through the "valley of death" which has killed many a start-up company. Perhaps there isn't a better testament to how loyal their customer base is than their volunteer bottling list.

Out of necessity, the brothers put the idea out there of having volunteers help them bottle their finished product. Initially, this approach was to simply save the cost of the salaries associated with employees who would only be needed sporadically as bottling needs occurred. What they have found is individuals like, make that love, being part of the production process of their favorite distilled spirits. Their list of a few friends and family members has now grown to over 300 people. These are individuals who not only like the fun of being involved in production, they buy Mississippi River Distilling Company's products. How cool is it to think you can go online after purchasing a bottle and look up the batch/bottle number and see yourself listed as the bottler of that particular distilled spirit?

It's something Mississippi River Distilling Company customers love, and the Burchett brothers appreciate as well. After all, they aren't working a road crew out in a hot Iowa summer.

They make whiskey for a living!

Mississippi River Distilling Company Photo Album

Ryan and Garrett Burchett

Mississippi River Distilling's Cody Road Bourbon

Mississippi River Distilling Company

The Rose

Making bourbon

Bottling

The team

Cheers!

Chapter 13
New Holland Artisan Spirits

66 East 8th Street
New Holland, MI 49423
(616) 355-6422

newhollandbrew.com
info@newhollandbrew.com

Established
1996

Leadership
Brett VanderKamp, Co-Founder & President

Product Lineup:
Bourbon(s)
Beer Barrel Bourbon

Other
Craft beer, Whiskey, Gin, Rum & Liqueur

"When I did this, I jumped in. You look back later and think, 'thank God I didn't know what I didn't know,' otherwise I might not have done it."
  -Brett VanderKamp

Gems and rocks, not barley and hops…

Brett VanderKamp was a hobby brewer. He didn't have visions of grandeur about opening a brewery and making a living selling beer as so many seem to, leading to their entry into craft brewing. He was too busy forging a career path as a geologist.

Even the course to becoming a geologist was a unique trip. Through high school, his plan was to become a doctor. He entered Hope College in Western Michigan his freshman year in pre-med. At the very start of his proposed future career as a doctor, he veered off path. He quickly discovered in his first biology class he didn't have a passion for what he had hoped would be his career.

He tried to power his way through it, grinding his way through that initial biology class, but Brett didn't have the fire it would take to go through the rigors of becoming a physician. Even if he forced his way through the years of schooling, could he actually be a doctor without an all-in passion for it?

After barely passing that first biology class, he knew he had to make a change. He worked with a counselor to figure out what the right career choice for him would be. He was seeking something he could wake up each day enthused about doing.

After many discussions and tests, Brett did land on something he got excited about: earth science. Hard rock geology and the study of ground water flow was something he was drawn to instantly.

With his educational focus now figured out, he jumped in with complete enthusiasm. Not that brewing wasn't an important part of his life. He had started in college and had even built his own homebrew system. Never, in his mind, though, was this anything beyond something fun to create and share with friends.

His hard work in college paid off when upon graduation he was offered a job in civil engineering in Colorado. A growing population with lots of new communities being built meant the State of Colorado would have a strong need for someone with Brett's skills for a long time to come.

Something had happened right around this time which made Brett once again question everything he was doing. His father, a chemical engineer and long-term employee for one of the largest and most well-known chemical companies in the United States, had lost his job near the tail end of his career. Through downsizing and corporate cuts, Brett's father and all of this father's friends lost their jobs at a time when they should be looking to retirement, not trying to find jobs to finish out their careers.

Seeing there wasn't such a thing as career safety hitting so close to home was eye-opening for Brett. After all, his father was a man who was very loyal to the company. Additionally, his dad possessed an enviable set of skills which would seemingly keep him employed at a company such as the one he had worked for.

Brett began to think about the fact the only way you can guarantee your future is to forge it yourself by being self-employed. While he was young and passionate, he didn't know exactly what type of business he could put this youth and passion behind.

He found his inspiration all around him in Colorado. Unlike his home state of Michigan where the major U.S. domestic brews still dominated, the craft brewing scene in Colorado was exploding. He had the benefit of not only seeing the tiniest of breweries making a go of it, but also players like New Belgium who had grown from a start-up to nationwide distribution.

Just as Brett had gone full bore when he transitioned from pre-med to focus on geology, he was going to take the same approach to entering the world of craft brewing. Without anything set, or even started back in Michigan, he put in his two-week notice at his job, packed up his Volkswagen Golf and moved back home to start on what would become New Holland Brewing.

While the company started out only as a craft brewery, Brett always had his eye on the world of distilled spirits as well. The main sticking point holding him back was simply the laws on the books in Michigan at the time. When they started in 1996, the cost for a distilled spirts license was $10,000 which would be almost impossible for a small craft distiller to make up.

By 2005, the landscape was beginning to change and the cost for the distilled spirits license had dropped to $1,000. It still took a few more years to get up-and-running, but by 2008, New Holland Artisan Spirits was born. They started in craft distilling with fruit-based spirits, utilizing old-fashioned pot distilling techniques and modifying early 20th century recipes.

By the time they got around to the notion of making a bourbon, they wanted to do something unique. Not the same old bourbon you find on the shelves.

New Holland's take on bourbon is fairly unique. Their brand is called Beer Barrel Bourbon. They start with a single malt whiskey made from 75% corn, 15% rye and 10% barley. Their product is then aged in bourbon barrels which have already been used to not only age bourbon, but their Dragon's Milk Bourbon Barrel Stout.

In the end, this gives Beer Barrel Bourbon another layer of creaminess and richness. It really rounds out the flavor and gives it a complexity you might find in a fine sherry.

Visitors to New Holland can enjoy tours where they discover both how to brew beer and distill spirits while sampling and drinking at the onsite pub/tasting room.

The future of New Holland lies in barrels. There is a lot to be explored with barrel aging still for them in both the brewing and distilling sides of the business. Brett has found consumers to be appreciative of the character and flavor profiles associate with the hard work and patience which goes into barrel-aged products.

A perfect example of what they are doing is with their Zeppelin Bend whiskey which is made of 100% malted barley and aged in charred oak barrels just like bourbon. It yields a slightly caramelized taste and an oak finish. Right now, it's the personal favorite whiskey of Brett himself.

Brett finds the most satisfying aspect of owning his own company goes beyond the freedom and career safety he set out to establish. The worries of having happen to him what happened to his father are long behind him. He likes the fact he has built a company where people can not only work, but a place they can also call home. Most importantly, they can contribute to the product their company produces.

Yep, as he looks back at his career choices, Brett VanderKamp has to agree that barley, hops, grains and barrels has a much better ring to it than rocks, groundwater flow and soil absorption!

New Holland Artisan Spirits Photo Album

Brett VanderKamp

Management team: Dave White (Operations), Fred
Bueltmann (Sales) & Brett VanderKamp

Barrels on the floor…

…and in the air

"The Pot"

Quality check

The final product

Customers enjoying the final product at New Holland

Chapter 14
Oregon Spirit Distillers

740 NE 1ˢᵗ Street
Bend, OR 97701
(541) 382-0002

oregonspiritdistillers.com
info@oregonspiritdistillers.com

Established
2009

Leadership
Kathy & Brad Irwin, Owners

Product Lineup:
Bourbon(s)
C.W. Irwin Straight Bourbon

Other
Vodka, Absinthe, Rum, Wheat Whiskey & Rye Whiskey

"Making great spirits is a craft you can learn but you will only excel at it if you have a passion for it."
        -Brad Irwin

A time-honored tradition in storytelling, whether it be in books, movies or TV, is the use of foreshadowing to engage and, sometimes, distract the audience. The writer, or director, alludes to the conclusion by giving hints along the way which begin to all make sense as the story comes together. Opening a distillery probably was always in the works for Brad Irwin; he simply needed to work through his own life story to have it all make sense for him.

In describing his jobs before opening Oregon Spirit Distillers with his wife Kathy in 2009, Brad refers to his career as a bunch of false starts. He simply couldn't find a job which brought out the best in him so he would grow bored and quit.

His fallback was always working at bars. Early in his career (the mid – late 80s), he was a bouncer. Every once in a while, his encounters were kind of humorous (like the time the group of over-served, attractive young women opened up some glow sticks and began showering the bar and other patrons with the contents), but for the most part, dealing with minors trying to sneak in and drunk patrons fighting wasn't any fun. Brad quickly transitioned to behind the bar where bartending was his go-to job between jobs.

In 2001, he met his future wife Kathy… at a bar (a drinking establishment is clearly the backdrop of the **Brad Irwin Story**, which will undoubtedly find its way to the Lifetime Network soon). She was out with a bunch of co-workers. He was on a date with someone else, but it wasn't going so well so he ended up joining what looked to be a much more fun and engaged outing.

After marrying in 2003, Brad and Kathy began thinking about a future a little bit more stable than a year or two of suit wearing, briefcase toting, robust 401k programs and benefits, corporate meetings, self-assessment about "What am I doing with my life?" and then back to bartending. The answer to what to do, finally became clear, and it truly was there the whole time. Open a distillery.

You may be thinking, "Is the foreshadowing from the fact Brad worked in bars?"

Well, that's part of the equation. The true interest in owning a distillery came more from Brad's approach to bartending than the fact he was actually doing it. What made Brad a great bartender was the fact he always got wrapped up in learning about the products he was serving. He wasn't the "tell me your problems" bartender. Nor was he the "flip the bottles Tom Cruise in *Cocktail*" type of bartender, either. Maybe you have to do a little bit of that stuff as a bartender, as it's just part of the job, but what truly made Brad stand out was his knowledge of distilled spirits.

Customers coming in and asking about what was a good bourbon or Irish whisky would find themselves in a mini-seminar complete with in-depth explanations of brands, quality overviews, process details, and best of all: tastings of different offerings. Brad began to have a clientele who looked to him for insight about new brands and his recommendations for distilled spirits based on criteria they provided in order for him to offer a brand which met their personal tastes. Brad's ability to make the perfect pick kept bringing customers back to him again-and-again.

By 2007, his passion for the process of distilled spirits grew to the point he began experimenting in his garage with making whiskey. Initially, his idea wasn't to do anything beyond to see if he could successfully make his own whiskey. In reality, this garage distilling was a look into a future he would realize very soon.

After some garage experiments, which ranged from bad to good to excellent, Brad began to think about opening a distillery. This would finally be his true calling and the idea of distilling resonated within deep inside of him from the moment he and Kathy began developing a business plan.

As any of the individuals profiled in this book can attest, opening a distillery is a challenge, and Brad and Kathy certainly had their fair share. In addition to the arduous amount of paperwork, they also had a problem with the name they originally wanted to use. Initial trademark searches came back clean on the name they wanted. Getting a name secured is a process which involves nets being cast further-and-further out, each step of the way. On the final search, after they had already gone far down the path of establishing their company under the name they wanted, a hit came up. This meant while someone had never used it as a distilled spirit company name, it had been used in some fashion. (It could be as simple as a mention in a promotion.)

Anyone who has been through this procedures knows the problems the Irwins were facing here. It's easy to make the case that nothing would ever happen. The name hadn't been used for a distilled spirits company, before so no one should try to step forward and claim the name. In reality, if this individual or entity ever did come forward, Brad and Kathy would more than likely have no problems in terms of legality but would be saddled with legal bills which could easily exceed $100,000 very quickly. In being frank, Brad and Kathy's lawyers told them as long as they were small, undoubtedly there wouldn't be an issue. Once they started expanding their horizons beyond their home base of Bend, Oregon, an unscrupulous person looking for a cash out, could try to make the case of their claim via litigation in hopes of a payday.

Brad and Kathy pondered what do for a while before deciding they needed a change. Their rationale was, "Why should we risk such a large amount of money defending what rightfully belonged to us?" Six figure legal bills wouldn't feel like much of a victory even if they did win. Plus, they knew they didn't have the money now and didn't want to risk it later even if they were successful at that point.

With all of this in mind, they began to search for a new name. Brad and Kathy kept going back to playing off of something with their home state of Oregon in it. The plan was to build a brand which featured locally grown grains. While Oregon isn't often recognized as a top producer for wheat, rye and barley, it does grow there and Brad is happy to stack it up against the raw materials produced anywhere. Plus, the State of Oregon is so associated with outdoors, natural beauty and environmentalism, Brad and Kathy felt it was already like a brand name by itself. They moved forward with the name Oregon Spirit Distillers. Once again, the Irwins might not have realized it at the time, but as they look back now, they realize the name was actually with them the whole time!

Getting started also involves raising capital. For many, the equity you give up can feel like a deal with the devil down the road as the payouts continue in perpetuity. However, after the payouts exceed the initial investment, the risk has gone away for the investors.

When Kathy and Brad were starting up, they needed a cash infusion for raw ingredients to make their product. Brad's brother Craig made a unique deal with them. Rather than taking an equity stake in the company, he would contract and pay upfront for two barrels of their bourbon. The deal got even sweeter when he clarified he would only need ½ of the product. The rest they could sell. This would give Oregon Distilled Spirits some much-needed funds, and it would give Craig some of their first whiskey. Craig would be able to enjoy it and give it out as gifts.

In exchange for this non-equity offering, Brad and Kathy surprised Craig by naming their bourbon C.W. Irwin Straight Bourbon after him (Craig Weber Irwin). It's a deal which runs "in perpetuity" but doesn't drain the company of profits as Brad and Kathy grow their business.

Best of all, Craig's namesake bourbon is truly something to brag about. Brad was very specific in formulating it. His mash contains 18% rye, 8% wheat and the balance being corn and some malted barley. The wheat blends the corn to the rye, but having the rye gives it a taste which is equally adept at enjoying neat while remaining bold enough to be mixed into cocktails.

The bourbon is aged in 53 gallon barrels (though they did initially start with 30 gallon barrels) with a #3 char, which is a medium char in the world of bourbon production. The final result is this perfect balance which achieves Brad's goals of being very smooth on its own while not getting lost in cocktails.

Brad notes that a business plan doesn't prepare you for what running a craft distillery is really like. Yes, it helps with the logistics of running and managing a business, just as it would with any other type of company you could run. The difference with a craft distillery is the personal connection and the relationships built in order to be successful. This is both with the obvious end user, their customers, but it also rings true with all of the other people behind the scenes, as well.

Brad didn't realize out of the gate how much time is spent fostering relationships with people like the farmers who grow their grains, service providers for other raw ingredients, distributors and wholesale customers. While he might not have prepared for this component, the relationships are now one of his favorite parts of being in the business.

Through the efforts of Brad, Kathy and their employees, Oregon Spirit Distillers truly connects with its customers. Visiting is a fun experience for taking tours, tasting samples and meeting the people who make the products being enjoyed. Once a quarter, Brad and Kathy offer workshops with curriculums including: mixology, spirit tastings, hands-on distiller training and holiday-themed drinks. They also offer an adopt-a-barrel program where your name is put on a barrel via a copper plate, you receive 24 bottles of the product from the barrel when it is ready and the ability to help bottle your product if you like. Plus, you get to keep the actual barrel. This program has proven to be especially popular with the expansive home-brewing community in Oregon as those home brewers love getting to own the barrel. They then use it to create their own bourbon barrel-aged beers.

The Oregon Spirits Distillery team is really starting to hit their stride. They have just moved into a new facility which will allow them to increase their production by three times. Brad and Kathy are as proud as they can be to not only provide a living for themselves, but eight other families who work for them as well (with more on the horizon as they continue to grow). They are in the process of rapidly expanding into other states and look forward to a future where they have expanded across the country.

For a guy who had so many "false starts" with his career, it's fun to see how well Brad is doing now that he has finally found something he loves to do for a living. At this point, Brad should be a master of seeking those moments in life which give hints of what you really should have been doing all along. We've already witnessed it here in his career choice; the garage distilling leading to owning a distillery, the name of his company and even the name of his bourbon.

These stories are nothing, though. Brad has one more that sounds like fiction but is completely true. One day he and Kathy were talking, and she was telling the story about a night in her youth, like 20 years before, when she and some friends were out drinking. They had glow sticks and for some reason decided it might be kind of cool to open them up and spray the contents in the bar. The bouncer threw them out. They quickly compared notes: where they were at that time in their lives, the location and even themselves, minus twenty years. Yep, it was them!

Now that is, without a doubt, the ultimate foreshadowing moment!

Oregon Spirit Distillers Photo Album

Brad and Kathy Irwin

Inside Oregon Spirit Distillers

Brad's brother Craig Weber (C. W. Irwin) has a bourbon named after him… literally his name! How cool is that?

Oregon Spirit Distillers product lineup

Chapter 15
Ozark Distillery

1684 Highway KK
Osage Beach, MO 65065
(573) 348-2449

ozarkdistillery.com
ozarkdistillery@gmail.com

Established
2012

Leadership
Dave Huffman, Head Distiller

Product Lineup:
Bourbon(s)
Ozark Distillery Bourbon

Other
Vodka and Moonshine

"One day I woke up and said, 'I'm going to open a distillery'."
  -Dave Huffman

America has a unique relationship with alcohol. When we read about the earliest settlers of our country, we learn about their struggles for the basics: food, water, clothing and shelter. While the history books in the classroom end with those items being secured, the "rest of the story" is that once those necessities were covered, the fifth item they secured was alcohol. Yes, it's true, America's early pioneers were brewing beer, making wine and distilling spirits!

The reopening of George Washington's distillery in 2012, helped remind us of the role alcohol had in our country's history. Like any long-term relationship, our bond with alcohol has had its rocky times as well. In fact, guilt of excess led to its ban during one of America's biggest legislative failures: Prohibition. The continued demand for the product by law-abiding citizens, combined with the growth of criminal syndicates providing illegally made hooch, meant lawmakers finally came to their senses and repealed Prohibition some thirteen years after it started.

Even though the Prohibition era ended over 80 years ago, the rules and regulations created to help repeal the amendment still loom large today for individuals seeking to enter the industry as well as private citizens. For example, while making wine and beer at your home for personal consumption is lawful, it remains illegal to make a drop of distilled spirits.

Although it continues to remain illegal to distill spirits at home, those who elect to shirk the law and set up their own still are not typically looked at as criminals if they are doing so for their own personal consumption… more like scoundrels.

Admit it. If you heard a co-worker made some really awesome backyard bourbon, you wouldn't be thinking about how you need to turn him in for criminal activity. You would be thinking about how you can get your hands on some of that sauce!

For more than 30 years, Dave Huffman was that guy. Yes, he was a scoundrel who knew it was technically illegal to run a small still in his home, but it was always for personal consumption. He truly liked the trial and error of working with the ingredients to refine his product.

As a young child, Dave grew up in Gardendale, Alabama, and later moved to Batavia, Iowa. He attended college at Emporia State University in Kansas where he met Tiffhany, his future wife. He graduated with a finance degree but never intended to work in the field of finance or banking. That may seem strange, but Dave always knew the base of knowledge he would acquire by getting a finance degree would prove invaluable in what he actually wanted to do: run his own business.

Both Dave and Tiffhany were pretty open to where they would live after graduation with one stipulation: they wanted to live on the water. They had friends who lived in the area surrounding the 55,000 acre lake in the center of Missouri known as Lake of the Ozarks. They had enjoyed visiting and spending time there over the years, so they ended up settling in Osage Beach, Missouri, a town at the center of the Lake of the Ozarks community.

Together, Dave and Tiffhany opened a real estate brokerage and found success selling property in this community which appeals to leisure enthusiasts from all over the Midwest. Their success as real estate brokers led to the opening of a second business, a property rental management company. As their second business began to grow and expand rapidly, they decided to focus solely on their new business, and they sold their real estate brokerage business.

When the economy began to struggle with the housing market crisis, Dave became concerned about having his family's livelihood tied up in a single business model solely based on consumer's discretionary income. While Lake of the Ozarks never suffered the same crippling real estate crash many other communities did during this time, it was looming large in Dave's mind.

When your brain works through scenarios enough, inevitably, thoughts leak into your subconscious. From there, they manifest themselves, and you don't know what's going to happen. Something bad might happen like getting an ulcer from nonstop worrying, or, conversely, something good might happen. For Dave, it was the latter.

One day, Dave awoke, and suddenly, the idea of what he needed to do for his future was completely clear. He needed to open a distillery. He knew the process well from his 30 years as a "scoundrel distiller." He clearly knew the business side of a start-up company from his background in finance and the two successful companies he had already started. Best of all, the alcohol business is always recession proof. In good times, people celebrate with alcohol; in bad times, they commiserate with it.

With Tiffhany's blessing, Dave proceeded with starting the distillery. Literally moving forward that day. He wakes up. His vision is clear. He explains his idea to Tiffhany. She's onboard. He's in the distilling business. He didn't spend months stewing over a business plan, spit-balling ideas on a white board and writing them out in a textbook version of "Starting a Business for Dummies" kind of way. He just jumped in. Plus, he had the space available at the facility where their property management company was housed, so he wouldn't have to run his ideas by a bank for approval. Dave figured he'd be busy enough filling out forms and paperwork for the government to enter into the distilled spirits business so the idea of taking time to outline a business plan just seemed like a waste of time for him.

Rejecting the conventional approach ended up being perfect for Dave. In fact, if he had written a business plan, with the benefit of hindsight, he realizes now it would have been all wrong. With a small facility, he would initially shun the idea of tours. He wanted to simply be "a guy making distilled spirits." That was his story. Not the process.

Despite the fact his entire process is confined to a 10' radius in their facility, Tiffhany pushed Dave to offer tours to discuss his process, and it was the key for Ozark Distillery really connecting with customers. Seeing how one person can create a product from raw ingredients to bottled product truly won over visitors to Ozark Distillery. It wasn't uncommon for people to spend over an hour in the 10' radius of the "distillery tour" and just be overjoyed with the idea of seeing how it works and talking with the person who makes all of it happen. Dave knew Tiffhany's logic was correct when he noticed that not only did almost every visitor pick up a bottle or two, these same people came back again-and-again to purchase his product and even take another tour.

Dave's bourbon offering, Ozark Distillery Bourbon Whiskey, is a wheated bourbon containing 60% corn, 20% wheat and 20% barley. He shirks the new-fangled approaches of additives and liquid enzymes designed to push the boundaries of efficiencies in the distilled spirits making process.

Despite the fact he owns a relatively young company, he adheres to the old fashioned approaches of spirit distilling he has crafted in his 30+ years of homemade hooch making. One area where his process differs from the large megabrand competitors is the fact he barrels a much cleaner alcohol. He boils off some of the bad alcohols which can negatively impact taste which the big guys leave in and let the barrel and time "mellow" those harsh flavors down.

His bourbon is a uniquely local offering perhaps unlike any other competitor in this segment. Not only are his raw ingredients locally sourced, even his barrels come from nearby Cuba, Missouri, where the cooper actually air dries the Missouri white oak staves for three years outdoors. Most barrel coopers speed up this lengthy process by drying their staves in a kiln, stripping away some of the natural flavorings picked up in the barrels.

The final product is packaged in a bottle made in Missouri, of course, and it is a smooth tasting bourbon with a nice sweet caramel taste.

Today, Ozark Distillery's one man and one woman operation is thriving. They are in 300+ stores and expanding. Their distillery business has been personally financed so they have been able to build their business without incurring debt. The Huffman's have recently decided to up the ante on their growth by ordering a larger still which will increase production by three times. All without a business plan.

So how have the Huffmans been so lucky? Dave points out there may be some other factors at work beyond just what he has done with the company.

His mother had been very ill as Dave and Tiffhany were starting the distillery. As he was getting ready to open, Dave had just been to visit his ill mother in Minnesota. He came back and filled his first bottles. With a Facebook post announcing they were in business with product to sell, the first customers came in to buy a bottle.

Soon after their first sales, the phone rang, and it was the doctor in Minnesota. He told Dave his mother was seriously ill, and it didn't look like she was going to make it. Dave questioned whether he would be able to make it there in time, and the doctor said he didn't think so. She passed away later that day, on the same day Dave sold those first bottles.

Dave, an admitted "mama's boy," feels a special connection to his mother with this business. He thinks about his mom with each successful step along the way.

So the question remains, how does Ozark Distillery have such success in the highly competitive world of distilled spirts? Well, it appears it starts with a great product, the dedication and hard work of the husband and wife team of Dave and Tiffhany Huffman and, yes, perhaps a little divine intervention from Mom!

Ozark Distillery Photo Album

The Huffman family

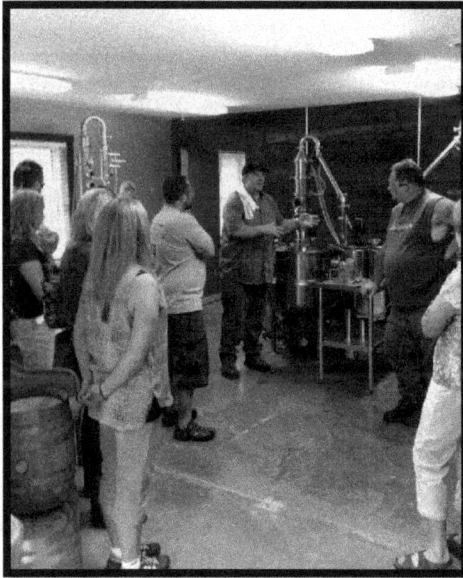

Dave delivering his famous 10' radius tour

Sample of some of the grains used to make Ozark Distillery's products

Infusing apple pie moonshine

Outside the distillery

Ozark Distillery product lineup

Chapter 16
Peach Street Distillers

144 South Kluge Avenue #2
Palisade, CO 81526
(970) 464-1128

peachstreetdistillers.com
info@peachstreetdistillers.com

Established
2005

Leadership
Rory Donovan, Bill Graham & Dave Thibodeau, Founders

Product Lineup:
Bourbon(s)
Colorado Straight Bourbon

Other
Vodka, Brandy, Grappa, Gin and Agave

"People have great stories of me waking up on their parking lot and brushing my teeth in my truck and then walking into their store to sell them my product back from the days when we were self-distributing."
   -Rory Donovan

Peach Street Distillers.

Clearly the best craft bourbon distillery in Georgia, right?

Well, if you were paying attention to the contact page, Peach Street Distillers is actually in Palisade, Colorado. The PSD team makes a pretty compelling argument why you may want to seek out Palisade peaches over the much more famous Georgia peach. We'll get to that story later, though. We'll begin this chapter with the story of Peach Street Distillers and the team behind the brand.

Had Rory Donovan not been a handful for his parents, Peach Tree Distillers likely would have never come to be. Rory grew up in northeast New Jersey. He felt his future was actually pretty clear, and it didn't involve opening a craft distillery in Colorado. He had recently dropped out of high school and accepted a job living on a boat as a fishing guide in Hawaii. He was going to get paid $100 a day plus tips. Living on the boat meant he had his housing needs taken care of and his job as a guide was doing something he loved: fishing.

What's not to like about this plan?

Plus, he had a quick comeback for every question his mother threw at him.

Mom: "Rory, this sounds great for now, but what are you going to do when you are an adult?"

Rory: "Mom, I live on the boat in Hawaii, and I make $100 a day plus tips."

Mom: "Fine. The problem is you are only thinking about right now. What are you going to do about retirement?"

Rory: "Mom, my retirement plan is I live on the boat in Hawaii, and I make $100 a day plus tips."

Rory's parents knew they weren't getting anywhere with the "living on a boat plan" so Rory's mother presented a deal to him. Before he went, she would spring for a 28 day outward bound rafting trip on the Green River in Colorado. It would work out great since he had an aunt living in Boulder. He could enjoy a fun trip and then visit family before heading to Hawaii.

True to her word, Rory's mom took him to Colorado for the rafting trip. He did have a great time, and he did get to visit with his aunt. It was there, at his aunt's house after a Bonnie Raitt concert, oddly enough, Rory's mother sprung the rest of her plan on him. She had enrolled him at the Colorado Timberlake Academy where he could complete his high school education. Nicknamed "Hoods in the Woods," the school catered to youths who had trouble with conventional high school. Rory's offer from his mother was to go to school, complete his diploma, and she would cover his expenses there and even pay for a skiing pass. After graduation, if he still wanted to go to Hawaii, she would buy the plane ticket. If he declined the offer, he was on his own and would need to pay his own way to Hawaii.

Rory elected to go with option A. He would stay in Colorado and complete his degree. He liked the idea of being able to ski every weekend, and the fact he had a backup plan of his parents paying for the trip to Hawaii if this didn't work out, was a bonus.

In the woods of Durango, Colorado, Rory Donovan did get back on track. Not only did he complete high school, he went on to college, attending Parsons School of Design, an art school back in the Northeast. He then settled back in Colorado where he worked at ski lodges in the winter and as a fishing guide in the summer.

With his background in art and outdoor culture, he hit it off with representatives from Orvis, the outdoor retailer while they were spending some time in Colorado for a convention. Rory submitted a tie design which was accepted by the company and remains in their catalog today, years later. He continues to collect residuals from the design with some years being better than others.

While working in Colorado he also met and befriended Bill Graham and Dave Thibodeau. Bill and Dave had opened Ska Brewing, a craft brewery in Durango. Rory enjoyed seeing the business grow and the behind the scenes work of brewing beer. In fact, he and Bill actually built their own still and started to experiment with distillation as a hobby.

When Ska Brewing got an invitation to attend a distillation workshop, Bill and Dave invited Rory to attend with them. Recent changes in the laws meant the concept of distilling in addition to brewing was appealing. Overall, the workshop was a disappointment. It turned to be more of a sales pitch than an educational workshop. In fact, the product they made during their time there was actually inferior to what Bill and Rory were making back home.

Still, there were some basics they were able to pull out of the workshop which helped them in establishing a plan to go in as partners and start their own distillery. The three opened up Peach Street Distillers in 2005. As one of the first craft distilleries in Colorado, the trio found it difficult to gain a footing in the marketplace. Distributors simply weren't interested in carrying a small brand which wasn't going to have the quick turns at the register the larger brands had.

With Bill and Dave having full time jobs running Ska Brewing, Rory took it upon himself to ensure Peach Street's products got on the shelves. He did it the only way he knew he would absolutely be represented properly: he loaded up a truck with product and drove all over the state of Colorado. Needing to conserve money meant he slept in the truck on overnight trips. He laughs when he looks back on those times now. Many store owners were charmed by the fact the owner of the company had spent the night sleeping in a truck on their parking lot to try to secure their business. He felt others were just trying to get him out of the store by offering to buy a case, thinking they would cancel when the distributor showed up with the product. They were surprised to see Rory carrying in a case of his product and an invoice a few minutes later.

Rory's hands-on approach worked. Peach Street Distillers soon had representation all over the state. He had even started distributing product for another Colorado-based craft whiskey distiller which helped cover the cost of the gas on his trips. Soon, the same distributors who wouldn't take his phone calls when the company was getting started were calling him wanting to represent his product in the marketplace.

When you have partners all with equal shares, but one doing all of the legwork, it isn't always harmonious. Rory points out there was a time when he likened what was happening with Peach Street to cancer. Either you can cut it out and address the issues, or you can leave it alone where it continues to grow and make the situation worse. Peach Street Distillers had a moment where it seemed like the company had cancer, and it would either recover or die. Luckily, the three owners worked through the issues, better defined everyone's role, and it has been a positive upward trajectory ever since.

Peach Street Distiller's Colorado Straight Bourbon is fairly unique in that the company is committed to delivering the tasting experience a customer would have enjoyed sipping bourbon two hundred years ago. Their first step in doing this is to cool down their mash with ice rather than letting it cool on its own. As far as the Peach Street team knows, they are the only ones to do this. This helps preserve the natural flavors of the raw ingredients.

Another differentiating factor they utilize is the fact they only run their product through the still one time. Again, they are not looking to "even out" the taste. They are looking to promote the idea of letting the ingredients come through in the flavor of their final product.

The final component they utilize to deliver a unique tasting experience to their customers is to prepare their raw ingredients in very small batches. For example, it takes three batches/still runs to fill one 53 gallon barrel. The Peach Street team feels these small batches help them offer a bourbon which is uniquely their own.

The team has landed on a mathematical approach to ensuring they have bourbon offerings at various ages. They age all of their bourbon a minimum of two years. They hold back 40% of their stock and then continue to age it another year. They will then retain 40% of that stock and age it another year. This approach allows them to offer products which have been in the barrel longer while retaining inventory for future releases.

The experience of visiting Peach Street Distillers really connects the company to its customers. They have a large bar area and a big patio outside. Weekends draw big crowds, and there are typically over a hundred people at any given time. Rory loves mingling with guests and never identifies himself as the owner. He loves the unfiltered feedback of guests simply talking about his products without knowing who he is.

The best part of the visiting experience is the fact the still is operated 24 hours a day right in the center of the room. The whole time people are visiting they are seeing production from the preparation of raw ingredients to bottling and packaging.

The future of the company is bright. They are at a time when they seem to be able to control how big they want to be. Their answer to "how big do we want to be" is "pretty big" since they have recently ordered a still which is four times the capacity of their current model.

Their future growth will come from their bourbon and their other products, as well. In addition to whiskey, Peach Street Distillers has a complete line of distilled spirits. Their product line includes brandy which utilizes the locally famous Palisade peaches, which give the company its name.

Palisade, Colorado, has a unique micro-climate. It is sunny almost ¾ of the year with a growing season of approximately half the year. The day and night temperatures swing wildly, dropping about 40 degrees when the sun goes down. These temperature changes mean the peaches' natural defense system is to become bigger and create more natural fructose and thus a larger and sweeter peach. Those in the know claim the "Palisade peach" is the sweetest and most delicious peach in the world.

That's how a distillery in the Western edge of Colorado became Peach Street Distillers.

Peach Street Distillers Photo Album

Rory Donovan

Outside Peach Street Distillers

Inside Peach Tree Distillers

Peach Tree Distillers' Colorado Straight Bourbon

Chapter 17
Silverback Distillery

9374 Rockfish Valley Hwy
Afton, VA 22920

sbdistillery.com
gorilla@silverbackspirits.com

Established
2014

Leadership
Christine Riggleman, CEO
Denver Riggleman III, Principal

Product Lineup:
Bourbon(s)
Blackback Bourbon

Other
Vodka, Gin, Whiskey and White Whiskey

"Kentucky started out as a part of Virginia. I'm just bringing bourbon back to its rightful home in Virginia."
-Christine Riggleman

The standard for any TV show or movie involves a format featuring "three acts." The first act is the introduction where the main characters are brought together, and the stage is set for the story. The second act involves an increase in action and a build up to the crescendo and resolution of the story. The third act is highlighted by the climax scene bringing the main story to a close. There may be further resolution of some subplots in a closing scene but the bulk of the show or movie is dedicated to those three acts.

The story of Christine and Denver Riggleman seemingly follows the formula of a three-act story with everything lining up for a happy ending for our main characters. That's not to say there isn't the potential for the story to change. In fact, like any good tale, there are bumps in the road which make it difficult for our hero and heroine to achieve a "Hollywood ending."

Let's take a look at a story, we'll call, *The Life and Times of Christine and Denver Riggleman*.

Act One
Christine and Denver Riggleman start off with an all-American story. They were high school sweethearts who ultimately got married. While Denver went to school, Christine worked in various jobs including a stint with NASA where she worked on the space station Freedom project. Denver then joined the Air Force, and he and Christine moved around the country. During this time, Christine stayed at home raising their three daughters, all born in different states. They viewed each move with an open mind

wondering if they may like the new location better than their home base of Virginia. Their plan, even back then, was to raise their family in the place they liked best out of all the stops they made.

Act Two

After leaving the Air Force, Denver decided to start his own business in the military defense contracting field. At this point, Christine and Denver knew they could live anywhere they wanted. Seeing so much of the country throughout their moves around the United States, they still felt like Virginia was home. They bought some land and built a home to raise their family.

Two major events occurred which would set the stage for the third act. First, Denver decided to sell his business. The cash from the sale, combined with the fact he continued to work full-time for the company which bought it, meant the Riggleman's had some discretionary money to pursue the dream of starting their own business.

Their only problem was they didn't know what their new opportunity might be. On a family vacation to Scotland, it suddenly became quite clear what Christine wanted to do. One of their stops was a distillery. During the tour they saw the entire process from start to finish and met the individuals making whiskey.

Being an artist in the kitchen, Christine saw it as an offshoot of what she was doing with her cooking. Plus, she began to calculate the potential of bringing a business like this to their hometown where over two million tourists a year visit.

After deciding to take the plunge as business owners in the distilled spirits industry, two pieces of family history came to light which made this venture seem like it was meant to be.

First, as Christine spoke to family members about starting this business, she was informed her great-grandmother had been in the business years before, albeit as a bootlegger, but in the business, nonetheless. It seemed that during Prohibition Christine's great-grandmother and her sisters had supplemented the family income during this time by producing and selling their own homemade gin. Denver also had a past which included a connection to bootlegging with family members having served as runners.

Secondly, Christine discovered she was related to the Carter family of Virginia, who are able to lay claim to having had the first winery in the United States (any industry going back three centuries is a little clouded as to where it got started but the Carters certainly are early on in the history of U.S. wine if they are, in fact, not the first).

It would appear the stage is set for act three!

Act Three

The idea for Christine's new venture would be a simple one built on conservation/ecology and catering to the tourism industry. The name they chose was Silverback Distillery based on the fact it was catchy, embraced their conservation mantra, and it was an inside joke/tribute to her husband. (Christine claims Silverback is the perfect nod to her husband. Let's look at the facts: He prematurely greyed giving him silver hair; he was a weightlifter so had the classic silverback build; he even has the attitude… seemingly a gruff exterior but is caring and protective of his family.)

With 50 acres, the Rigglemans would be able to build right on their existing property. In order to lower their impact on the environment, Silverback became the first distillery to use a geothermal system to heat and cool water. To accomplish this, over 5 miles of piping was trenched 8 – 10 feet deep. The end result was a large upfront cost but, in-turn, a unique system which also increased efficiency by taking a two-hour task of heating or cooling water and whittling it down to only 5 – 15 minutes using their geothermal approach.

In order to get up-to-speed on what they needed to create their distilled spirits, they hired an operations manager. Christine and he began an apprenticeship at a well-known distillery. Learning while apprenticing was invaluable. They felt like they were able to take the best of what that company offered and gained insight into other areas which needed improvement.

In addition to vodka, gin and white whiskey, which can be brought to market very quickly since they do not have to be aged, Christine wanted to get in the bourbon business. Reading the trade magazines, she knew there was a shortage of bourbon. Increased interest in the product domestically and internationally meant there would be a strong demand for bourbon in present and the future.

With companies trying to meet this increased demand, the industry had begun to also suffer from a shortage of barrels which are used to age the product. Initially, Christine and Denver thought they might be to open their own cooperage to build their own barrels but quickly realized the lack of barrels was due to lack of wood utilized and not companies willing to make them.

The smooth-talking Christine was able to make a contact at Independent Stave Company, a leading barrel manufacturer. Christine notes that once you get on their list of partners, you are golden! They treat all of their customers the same whether they are a multi-billion dollar international company or a small start-up like her. This relationship has been invaluable in getting Christine into the bourbon business.

Currently, Christine's Blackback Bourbon is aging. Her slightly sweet mash should yield a bourbon which is an easy drinking whiskey.

Getting to where she is today has not been easy. The first hiccup came with two lawsuits challenging the trademark of the name Silverback Distillery. The first lawsuit was thrown out but the second involved a company outside of the industry which had once run a promotion with a beer company. Rather than exhaust resources in fighting the matter in court, the Rigglemans elected to keep the name of the company Silverback Distillery but brand the products under their own unique names. Their gin goes under the name Strange Monkey, their vodka Beringei (the scientific name for the breed of gorilla commonly known as the "Mountain Gorilla") and their bourbon/whiskies under the name Blackback. (The rest of the male gorillas in the family under the leadership of a "silverback.")

This still left them with the issue of having an SB on their label design. It had been for Silverback but in a Riggleman family collaborative effort one of their daughters, Lillian, came up with the idea that it would now stand for the "Spirit of Beringei."

Another issue has been the financing of their business. The two million dollar investment in her facility has been funded exclusively by the Rigglemans without any help from the state. No grants. No tax breaks. No sweetheart loans.

This issue has been exasperated by the early success of Silverback Distillery. Under Virginia law, 15% of sales for a small business like Silverback are retained by the State in a pool which the company can in-turn use for expenses like supplies or payroll. Within a month-and-a-half, their sales numbers exceeded the threshold for the 15% retention and it was cut to 10%. Future growth will likely eliminate it altogether which is challenging for a business just getting off of the ground.

Of course, cash flow is an issue in a controlled State like Virginia. Alcohol sales all go to the State and then, 30 – 60 days, later they pay Silverback. With the company carrying the money for up to 60 days, the Rigglemans are basically floating the State a loan with every bottle sold, so cash flow is always an important resource Christine must manage.

The final issue facing the Rigglemans in this third act is one which is looming large over them right now. Currently, there is an environmental study taking a look at the impact of adding 42" natural gas pipelines in the area. One plan brings the pipeline right through their property. Without the details of the study, or the plan, the Rigglemans are unsure of what impact this will have on them. It could mean nothing, it could be minimal or, at the other end of the spectrum, it could possibly mean they have to shut their doors.

The Rigglemans aren't harping on the "what ifs," though. They know they have a winner on their hands with Silverback Distillery and plan to go into contingency planning should there be a need.

In just six short months, they have received approval for three states. Their short-term goals involve continued expansion with the ultimate goal of being in all fifty states as well as markets abroad.

It appears Christine and Denver have set the stage for a happy ending to this story!

The End!
(Camera fade out.)

Silverback Distillery Photo Album

Christine Riggleman

It's rare to have a customer NOT take a photo by
Silverback's chainsaw carved full-size silverback gorilla

Silverback trademarked this phrase to celebrate the release
of their Strange Monkey Gin

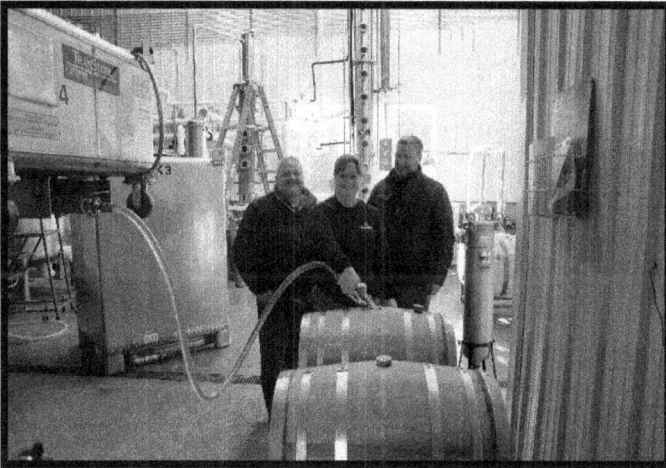

Denver (left) and Brad the Assistant Operations Manager
(right) watch Christine fill the first barrel of whiskey

Chapter 18
Syntax Spirits

625 3rd Street, Unit C
Greely, CO 80631
(970) 352-5466

syntaxspirits.com
info@syntaxspirits.com

Established
2010

Leadership
Heather Bean, Co-Founder

Product Lineup:
Bourbon(s)
Syntax Spirits Bourbon

Other
Vodka, Whisky and Rum

"I look at everything through an 'abstract engineering' approach."
-Heather Bean

A craft distiller making bourbon, vodka, rum and whisky... is the name actually Syntax or is it Sin Tax? Well, we will take a look at the company name in a bit, but first let's see how it got started.

With degrees in both chemical and mechanical engineering, career options are pretty vast. Fresh out of college, dual-degreed Heather Bean took the safe, stable and conventional approach and went to the corporate world. By most accounts, you would say Heather had it pretty good. She had a job in her field of training with a respected company, making good money.

That would be the evaluation from "most accounts."

Heather's assessment of her career was a little different: it was boring! The corporate life... meetings, office politics, the "ground hog's day" reality of a corporate job all added up to simply not being fun or fulfilling to Heather. Rather than making a career shift, Heather decided if she could spice up her personal life, perhaps it could make her work life more tolerable. She turned to what every corporate type does for recreation. Golf? Yoga? Biking?

Nope. Kayak polo.

Okay. Admittedly, most people do not turn to kayak polo in this same situation. Heck, most people don't even know what kayak polo is (though the words kayak and polo, while not traditionally married together, are pretty descriptive as to what the game actually is when connected to one another).

Then again, unlike Heather, most of us aren't some sort of Justice League superhero with degrees in mechanical and chemical engineering so kayak polo actually sounds like the perfect way to blow off some steam for her.

So, it's true. Heather, who began running a regional kayak polo league, met Jeff Copeland at a league event. Jeff was just returning from a stint living in New Zealand and wanted to meet some new people. You're probably wondering if this leads to the start of Syntax Spirits. She meets Jeff, who has a deep family history and work career in distilled spirits, at kayak polo, they develop a friendship, and it goes from there. Well, Jeff and Heather did meet at kayak polo, but Jeff didn't have a craft distilling background. Actually, he's an atmospheric scientist.

That completes the trifecta needed for any great distillery: mechanical engineering, chemical engineering and atmospheric science.

While the path to starting Syntax may seem unconventional, the truth of the matter is the seedlings for this business had been planted all the way back in the late 80s soon after they met at kayak polo. Jeff had homebrewed as a hobby. As a child, Heather watched her mother make wine so she started with wine making and then moved onto brewing. She had even considered opening up a brewery out of college but with a microbrewery boom going on in Colorado at the time, it seemed like the market was already saturated. Thus, she took the more "conventional" career path with her corporate job.

As she began her time of self-reflection and evaluation of her career, coming to terms with the idea of needing to do something different, she had taken note of the craft distillery movement during her travels for work. Back home in Colorado, there weren't yet many companies getting into the artisanal world of craft distilling.

Over time, as the friendship grew, Jeff and Heather had started sharing their love for creating something uniquely their own by brewing together. They then decided to take a chance at starting a business together. It was comforting for both of them to be able to bounce ideas off of another person. Plus, it would have been difficult to provide a living for both of them as a start-up. Luckily, Jeff was happy in his job, so Heather would take on the day-to-day responsibilities of running the business, and Jeff would be able to continuing working in the atmospheric science field but be available for business and financial decisions and help out on an ad hoc basis.

The name for their company, Syntax Spirits, was a play on words. As a writer of both words (an occasional author) and computer code (in her job), Heather like the dual play of how it fit in both. (Syntax being the principles of sentence structure in linguistics and the rules of code writing/ construction in computer programming.) Plus, both she and Jeff liked the name Syntax as a nod to the taxes they pay to make their product (distilled spirits taxes are often jokingly referred to as "sin tax" along with other taxes paid on items consumed strictly for luxury/enjoyment).

Getting started was challenging. There were good challenges and bad ones. On the good side, ever the engineer, Heather enjoyed the build out of the facility. Conceptualizing the vision of your working distillery and then building and installing the equipment, for Heather, it was a Saturday night type of fun every day of the week.

Dealing with multiple government agencies at the local, state and federal levels to get a craft distillery going? Well, that's not much fun for anybody! Plus, while testing off the charts in all things engineering doesn't mean you know everything about every component of running a business. She struggled with the paperwork/bookkeeping side of her company. Luckily, her retired mother had been a career bookkeeper. She was able to provide insight and consultation to ensure Heather stayed on track, took care of all tax information and got all of the bills paid on time (Just because Heather wasn't a numbers genius doesn't diminish her superhero status... even Superman has his kryptonite.)

Like most distilled spirits manufacturers, Syntax's first offering was vodka (vodka is always the quickest distilled spirit which can be brought to market). Knowing aging would take some time, Sytnax Product Manager Ryne Sherman convinced Heather to get started working on what would become Sytnax Spirits Bourbon right away. The bourbon recipe Ryne and Heather came up with is a wheated bourbon. Their mash is made up of locally sourced grain and is comprised of 51% corn, 40% wheat and 9% barley. They age their product in full-sized barrels so as to not rush the aging process. It takes about a year for their product to start to take shape and begin to taste like bourbon. After another year in the barrel, the two-year-old product's flavor really begins to balance out. They are left with a nice clean spirit with a smooth finish. The taste of the wheat is leveled out nicely by the oak in the barrels.

Heather's touch can be found all over Syntax Spirits, not just in their product. When she's not working in the distillery, or involved in managing the business, she's busy building. Not just little projects like a handle fell off of a cabinet. We're talking grand-scale metal works: machine tool, get out the arc welding set and that cool hat that flips down over your eyes as you snap your head down when that fiery, burny thing gets lit with the neat little gizmo which creates a spark.

In addition to an industrial feel in the large tasting room, the works of several local artists are displayed. This is a rotational exhibit with new artists constantly being showcased. Their clientele runs the gamut from college students to retirees with all age groups seemingly equally enjoying the experience of a visit.

The most satisfying aspect of running the business for Heather is just seeing all of it work. Like everything in life, her distillery is a large engineering equation. Sure, there are many individual components to it, each with unique processes needing to function to make things work, but when it all comes together to produce these incredible distilled spirits her customers enjoy, Heather couldn't be any happier. (Yes, despite the busy schedule of running her business, Heather continues to be involved in running the local kayak polo league. Jeff has moved on from kayak polo to Aikido where he is now a third degree black belt.)

In terms of the future, Heather sees slow, obtainable growth. Heather would like to see her brand expand from a local offering in Colorado, fanning out regionally before it continues to slowly grow beyond their immediate area. A large scale growth spurt would stretch their ability to maintain quality standards, and it isn't an approach Syntax sees as a viable way to keep delivering the experience their customers are used to. Plus, she can't get too big where she doesn't have time to fill in for the Justice League when Wonder Woman calls in sick!

Syntax Spirits Photo Album

Jeff Copeland and Heather Bean

Where it all started... kayak polo!

Wonder Woman!

Some of Heather's handy work: A gate designed by Heather and Production Manager Ryne Sherman to separate the production area and tasting area.

Gustav is the greeter and goodwill ambassador at Syntax

He's even got a product named after him (Big Cat Light Whisky)

Gustav isn't the only one with a label design. Well-known pinball artist Greg Freres does all of Sytnax's label work. He fashioned the vodka label after Heather. She claims with enough bourbon consumption it's a dead ringer for her! ☺ (Notice the kayak polo paddle)

Syntax Spirits Bourbon

Chapter 19
Thumb Butte Distillery

THUMB BUTTE

D I S T I L L E R Y
Prescott • Arizona

400 N. Washington Avenue
Prescott, AZ 86301
(928) 443-8498

thumbbuttedistillery.com
thumbbuttedistillery@gmail.com

Established
2013

Leadership
Dana Murdock, Jim Bacigalupi, Scott Holderness & Mario Passalacqua, Owners

Product Lineup:
Bourbon(s)
Bloody Basin Bourbon

Other
Gin, Vodka, Rum, Rye and Single Malt Whiskey

"We have found others in this industry to be very willing to help. They treat you like colleagues instead of competitors."
-Dana Murdock

Imagine, for a moment, you were named CEO of a **Fortune 500** company where the Board of Directors had just cleaned house and fired the entire management staff. Your first order of business would be to hire the right team. This is no small task as you are not just looking for the best people, you need to find experienced specialists to ensure the future success of the company. For instance, just because someone appears competent, and even has an advanced degree of business acumen, it doesn't necessarily mean you could just plug them in as your Chief Financial Officer. That position requires a specialist. Someone who has the education and work experience, combined with the competency skills, to flourish in that particular position.

Most small start-up businesses do not have benefit of having a management team with diverse backgrounds to help the company achieve its goals. Instead, they tend to start with the vision of one person who then does his or her best to learn each of the skills needed to get their businesses going. Typically, as the company grows, a management team of experts is then built up over time.

Thumb Butte Distillery, Arizona's first distillery since Prohibition ended, has been able accomplish an unbelievable amount of success in a very short time. They are currently Arizona's only distillery offering a complete line of products. From gin, vodka, rum, whiskies and their Bloody Basin Bourbon, Thumb Butte Distillery has a product catalog of which distilleries in the business for twice as long as they have been would be envious.

It all goes back to the owner/management team. Four friends from very different backgrounds, each bringing a unique skill set which would elevate Thumb Butte in very short order. The kind of individuals sought to lead the **Fortune 500** company in the above scenario.

Think about this, if you are starting a distillery, you need to have someone with experience running a business. They are going to need both retail and wholesale application as they will likely be in contact directly with consumers at your facility and understanding of wholesale and distribution channels to get your product to market. You are going to need to stand out from the crowd so someone with an artistic background is a plus to help design your labels and build a brand identity. Obviously, it all starts with the science and artistry of creating a product so a person with a background in brewing or distilling is key. Finally, owning a distillery involves a lot of equipment and a build out which maximizes efficiency for the small scale and limited resources of a new company.

Now, check out these résumés:

Dana Murdock – For over 10 years, Dana Murdock owned and operated an artisan bakery and restaurant in Southern California. Her business also included a wholesale component in which she supplied bread to local merchants for their businesses.

Jim Bacigalupi – Graduating with a fine art degree specializing in furniture design, Jim's master thesis was a custom bar design and build out in Los Gatos, California. After completing several more bars, he began to get work for the Catholic Church. When Pope John Paul II came to the United States in 1987, Jim was commissioned to design and build the furniture for the Masses during the trip. Jim built over 40 pieces including Pope John Paul's chair and the altar used. His pieces were used in the Masses the Pope led on the visit, including the famous one at Candlestick Park in San Francisco, which was attended by over 70,000 people. These pieces reside today at St. Mary's Cathedral in San Francisco.

Scott Holderness – A retired physician, Scott used his knowledge of science in a different application for his hobby of home brewing beer. His passion went beyond simply experimenting himself. Scott took classes both on brewing and distilling to learn more about the science and artistry of creating his own home brews.

Mario Passalacqua – A mechanical engineer with experience working for both Anheuser-Busch and Miller, Mario also was self-employed in property development and custom home building.

The journey of Thumb Butte Distillery began with Dana working as a ceramics instructor at the local college in Prescott. She was bored with the simplicity of the job and wanted something more challenging. She was striving for something more. Something which actually contributed to the community in which she lived.

She had met Scott at one of her classes. She had met Jim at a music class she was also taking. She played guitar, and he played piano. Mario, an old friend back in California where she had run her bakery/café, had moved to Prescott, as well.

As the friendship grew for the four, the idea of starting a business together began to be discussed. As they evaluated the individual specialties of each, the collective strength of the team seemed well-suited to run a distillery so Dana began crafting a business plan.

Not only were the four out of "central casting" for their respective roles in starting a distillery, Prescott, Arizona, their home base, had a long history going back to the days of the Wild West as a place to find a locally made distilled spirits. With the entire industry disappearing over time, culminating with Prohibition closing everyone down, an area once known as "Whiskey Row" had no companies making distilled spirits.

Dana's plan was to capitalize on this rich history by focusing the brand on the area, starting with the company name. Thumb Butte refers to the volcanic plug geographic formation which sticks up right in the middle of town. It literally looks like a thumb and can be seen from anywhere in town.

The home for their company came from Jim Bacigalupi. He owned a building which had served as the headquarters and studio for his once thriving custom design furniture company. While business had boomed in the 70s and 80s, the 1990s saw less people buying custom furniture, and his business began to wane. Starting a distillery in a furniture studio meant a major overhaul to the building, but luckily Mario Passalacqua had experience in building and engineering so he took a hands on approach by taking the lead on this aspect of getting Thumb Butte going.

The company also had a head start on developing their product with Scott Holderness' history in brewing. While distilling is certainly different than brewing, the basics are all there. Plus, all distilled spirits truly start as beer prior to getting distilled, so the learning curve on beginning was much lower for the Thumb Butte team than it was most companies just starting out.

As the company began producing products, they continued to feature the local history by utilizing names which tied into Prescott. Their Gurley Street Gin is named after a street which runs straight through town. Their Central Highlands Single Malt is named after the fact Prescott is in the center of Arizona, and their altitude is a mile high. Their Rodeo Rye is named after the fact Prescott is home to the oldest rodeo in the United States.

Their Bloody Basin Bourbon is also named after a historic 1873 battle in the area between the U.S. Army and a tribe of Indians. Once again, Dana likes to highlight this local connection by sharing the local history with the "story" she crafts and puts on the bottle. Here is description of the Battle of the Bloody Basin, taken right from the bourbon bottle:

Bloody Basin Bourbon
Just southeast of Prescott off Interstate HWY 17 lies Bloody Basin. This was the location of a reprisal attack by the military against a band of Tonto Apaches.

In March of 1873 this band of Tonto Apaches attacked and killed a party of three settlers. This attack by the Tonto spurred a strong reprisal by Captain George Randall who was under the general command of General George Crook.

They located the Tonto Apaches at Turret Peak, a Yavapai stronghold. Randall and a group of soldiers and scouts crept up Turret Peak at

*midnight, and at dawn they attacked. The
Apaches were taken by surprise and many
jumped to their death off the precipice. The rest
were killed or surrendered. The number of
Apaches killed varies by account from 26 to 57.
After this incident the Apache resistance quickly
dissipated and most of the Tonto band was
resettled to the San Carlos Reservation, not to
return for many years.*

*We hope that our Bloody Basin Bourbon inspires
you to take an interest in the history of our region
and the West as a whole. You will find it
fascinating, and we will help you through any
sinking spells. Take a pull from your Thumb
Butte Flask, read the history, and try to accept
the shared fault, ambiguity and guile from all
players.*

The grain for Thumb Butte Distillery's bourbon is locally
sourced and has a mash of 70% corn and the balance of rye
and malted barley. They age their bourbon in a variety of
barrels including 5, 10 and 53 gallon barrels.

For those not educated about the topography and varying
climates of Arizona, you may wonder about the impact the
weather of Prescott has on the aging process for Thumb
Butte's bourbon offering. The dry climate in the mile high
altitude of Prescott does swing wildly depending on the time
of the year. Their winter lows hover around zero, and their
summer highs get into the 90s, meaning they have the ideal
situation of their product expanding in and out of the wood in
their charred oak barrels.

Their finished product is a smooth tasting rye-based bourbon. A sampling of Bloody Basin Bourbon is often likened to high end offerings from the large Kentucky distilleries, which makes the team at Thumb Butte pretty pleased, taking into considering the short amount of time they have been distilling in comparison to the big boys.

Of course, would you expect anything less than perfection from a team like the four business "rock stars" of Dana Murdock, Jim Bacigalupi, Scott Holderness and Mario Passalacqua?

If you ever do get a call to manage a **Fortune 500** company where the entire management team has been let go, it's probably a good idea to give those four a call!

Thumbe Butte Distillery Photo Album

Dana Murdock & Jim Bacigalupi

Scott Holderness & Mario Passalacqua

Inside Thumb Butte Distillery

You get a front row view of production at Thumb Butte

Thumb Butte Bloody Basion Bourbon Whiskey

Chapter 20
Woodstone Creek Winery & Distillery

WOODSTONE CREEK
ARTISAN WINERY & DISTILLERY

4712 Vine Street
Cincinnati, OH 45217

woodstonecreek.com
woodstonecreek@yahoo.com

Established
1997

Leadership
Don Outterson, Owner

Product Lineup:
Bourbon(s)
Woodstone Creek Straight Bourbon Whisky

Other
Wine (white, red and dessert), Mead (ranging from dry to sweet and dessert), Vodka, Single Malt Whiskey, Blended Whiskey, Bierschnapps, Unaged Whiskey and Gin

"I know how to be successful and small."
-Don Outterson

When upstate New York native Don Outterson entered the workforce, he knew exactly the industry where he wanted to make a career: beer. He had been brewing beer in his spare time and had met a lot of people in the business through this hobby. He had managed to garner their attention with some of the beers he created, and one of his brews won the New York State Amateur Championship.

The idea of working with the watered down uniform taste of American lagers didn't generate a whole lot of excitement for him, though. Outterson, a descendant of Northumbrian Scots, decided to go back to his roots and explore the idea of educating himself on the European approach to brewing.

Through a contact he had gained while homebrewing, he was able to land an apprenticeship in cask conditioned English Ales at a brewery in Albany, New York. His mentor in Albany had trained under noted brewer Peter Austin at the Ringwood Brewery in Kent, England. Years later, Austin would create a legacy in American brewing by selling equipment to microbreweries as the burgeoning craft brewery revolution began to gain traction. Today, many breweries still utilize his Ringwood Ale Yeast.

Don found the approach to brewing to be completely different than what he had found in America, not only the small finite details, but even at the macro level. For instance, in America, brewing and distilling is considered industry. Raw ingredients are sourced on the futures market as commodities.

In Europe, brewing and distilling is considered agriculture. Raw ingredients in an English ale or Scottish whisky are as important in the process as the artistry of preparing them. Specific recipes wouldn't call for "grains" or "wheat," they would be grains or wheat grown in a specific region and might even be further clarified by harvest times. A spring harvest could potentially have a different flavor profile than a fall harvest. In America, we see this level of dedication to raw ingredients in the wine industry (where it is classified as "agriculture") but not in brewing and distilling.

The education Don received in English ales, via his apprenticeship, would inspire him to try to introduce this approach and dedication to ingredients via his creations.

After finishing his apprenticeship, he secured a job at a Utica, New York, brewery working for a Canadian brewmaster. He was able to not only learn the business side of running a brewery, but also he picked up brewing tips on the process of Canadian lagers. During his time in Utica, his mentor nominated him into membership to the Master Brewer's Association of The Americas.

Wanting to further his education, Don decided to attend the prestigious Siebel Institute of Technology in Chicago, a brewing school opened in 1872. Upon graduating he began to look for an opportunity to lead a brewery/brew pub as the brewmaster.

Through a contact, Don heard about a brewery start-up in Minneapolis. He spoke to the owner and was able to negotiate salary/employment details over the phone. While it sounds crazy now, in the time before we had the information of the internet, his only knowledge of the company was through the owner over the phone. When Don got there, he was surprised to see that not only was he coming to a start-up company, it literally hadn't "started up" at all. It was more of just a concept.

He had two choices. He could turnaround and head back to New York or stick around and try to build a business. Don elected to do the latter which involved a complete build out of a brewery. Anyone who has ever opened a brewery will tell you one of the most difficult aspects is the planning and build out as it impacts the process and efficiency in which you will work from that point forward. Again, this was completely unexpected, but it was an impactful portion of Don's education.

He ended up staying in Minneapolis long enough to not only get the business going, but to land them gold, silver and bronze medals for their beers at the Great American Beer Festival.

Don's next stop was a brewpub in Chicago before turning to another side of the business, selling equipment and ingredients to brewers/brewpubs which seemed to be popping up everywhere. He also supplemented his income by doing some writing for **American Brewer Magazine** and serving as distilling editor for **American Brewer and Distiller Magazine**.

Through contacts made in his writing jobs, he was able to land a job for an Australian Development company which wanted to join the brewpub revolution in the United States. While working for them in Cincinnati, he met Linda, whom he would fall in love with and eventually marry.

Like the rest of Don's story, it didn't happen easily. The brewpub idea in the U.S. wasn't working out for the

Australian company, so they closed up shop on those projects and brought Don to Australia to work. For a guy who initially had just wanted to bring a European approach to brewing back in upstate New York, he now found himself on the other side of the world, far away from the woman he loved back in Cincinnati.

After finishing his contract, Don decided to leave Australia and head back to Cincinnati and Linda. Rather than working for someone else, Don knew it was time for him to take all of the knowledge he had gained and utilize it in starting his own company. He considered opening a brewery, but the first round of craft breweries and brewpubs was waning. Also, the licensing was cost prohibitive for a person looking to get going on a shoestring. A license to brew beer in Ohio was $3,700, and he and Linda would need a second $3,700 license to serve beer (something pretty important at a brewpub). The cost for a license to open a winery was $125. That was an all-in cost in that this single license gave them the right to produce wine, offer tastings and sell/distribute it.

The plan for Linda and Don initially was a traditional winery. Because the wine industry is considered agriculture (like the brewing and distilling industries in Europe), the State of Ohio was regulating which grapes could be used in their product. Don and Linda found the grapes they were being directed to utilize grew easily in the area, but they didn't yield the flavor profiles they were looking for.

Don's idea was to turn to mead. Mead is a honey-based alcohol drink which draws upon brewing techniques from beer production as well as some of the subtleties of winemaking. While it is often most associated with beer/brewing, it does take the flavor profiles of wine (from dry to sweet) and, most importantly, was covered under the $125 wine license Don and Linda had already secured.

Needing to keep an eye on the budget, Don and Linda needed a place where the overhead wasn't going to kill their fledgling business. Don found a 75 year old farmer who was semi-retired still doing a little bit of farming with his 103 year old mother. They had an extra barn, so he was able to set-up shop there with minimal overhead. As the "young guy" on the farm, he would have to jump in and help out with some of the chores, in particular, if it involved heavy lifting.

Mead proved to be the perfect entre for Don and Linda into the market. It was different enough to gain attention for both wine and beer drinkers looking for something new. Plus, mead didn't have some of the baggage and preconceived notions attached to it they likely would have encountered had they attempted to open a traditional winery.

As their business grew, Don and Linda began to expand into wine and then distilled spirits.

Distilled spirits meant a whole new education for Don. Like everything, he learned by educating himself, not through the internet or books, but instead by attending the Alltech Alcohol School in Nicholasville, Kentucky, for his formal education and speaking to people who distilled for a living for his informal learning plan. He found the master distillers in the whiskey-making business in Kentucky to be particularly engaging and open to providing advice.

One of the best parts about speaking to bourbon distillers is the fact they would provide advice and recommendations on how to make a product better, even if they weren't doing it themselves. While most of the companies making bourbon have been taken over by large multinational companies with an eye on the bottom line, they employ master distillers who know the tricks and shortcuts to save money but diminish the quality of the product.

As they would walk Don through the process of making bourbon, they would start out a conversation with a statement, "What you need to do is…" and conclude it with, "…but we don't do that here." The whole time Don's making mental notes about what they are doing that works as well as what they *aren't* doing that works, too.

This education from some of the most well-known and respected companies in the bourbon business helped Don when he was formulating Woodstone Creek Straight Bourbon Whisky, his foray into the market. Of course, Don wasn't satisfied with using just what he was taught. He employs a personal philosophy of, "If you are going to the trouble of making it, your product has to have the benefit of your own expression."

You simply can't have a product which tastes exactly like everyone else's!

Don crafts his bourbon offering with three pillars:

1). It's a single barrel product
2). It's double pot-stilled
3). It's triple-malted.

The end result is a smooth-tasting bourbon not only appreciated by his customers but recognized by the Beverage Tasting Institute, as well.

Don and Linda have long since outgrown the "barn on the farm" where they got started. In fact, they moved out of there after a few years and into a building owned by a friend. They spent thirteen years there but when the other business occupying the building needed to expand, they once again found themselves without a home for their company. Luckily, a spot in a building for their current home on Vine Street opened up. This allowed Don and Linda to make "wine on Vine."

They have an excellent production facility, an upscale tasting room and plenty of room to grow at their current location. Don continues to be motivated by the expression of satisfaction delivered to customers by his creations. He cites the love of the fact you are never finished learning in this business as the big motivator for him to continue to evolve.

Don has plans to go back to his roots and begin brewing beer again very soon. He will then have all bases covered.

Whether you want a beer, distilled spirit, wine or mead, Woodstone Creek will have a product for you!

Don Outterson

The Tasting Room at Woodstone Creek

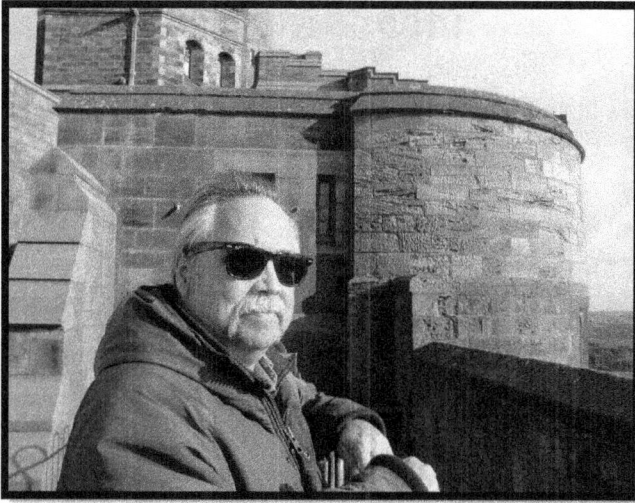

Don at Baumburgh Castle (in England) – This castle was built on the foundation of Utred's Castle, which had belonged to ancestors of Don's when the land belonged to Scotland

The first label for Woodstone's Bourbon and an updated look

Author's Notes/Resources

One of the greatest aspects about writing these books is meeting all of the great people behind the brands. Their personal stories, along with the stories of their businesses, continue to offer fascinating insight about owning a small brand in America today. Of course, writing about a subject as fun as bourbon doesn't hurt either!

I encourage you to learn more about these individuals and their businesses. To make your job a little easier, here's a recap of the websites for each:

2bar Spirits – *2barspirits.com*

10th Mountain Whiskey & Spirit Co. – *10thwhiskey.com*

Barrel House Distilling Co. – *barrelhousedistillery.com*

Black Dirt Distillery – *blackdirtdistillery.com*

Cedar Ridge Vineyards & Distillery– *crwine.com*

Colorado Gold Distillery – *coloradogolddistillers.com*

Coulter & Payne Farm Distillery – *coulterandpaynefarmdistillery.com*

Dark Corner Distillery – *darkcornerdistillery.com*

Grand Traverse Distillery – *grandtraversedistillery.com*

Heritage Distilling Co. – *heritagedistilling.com*

Journeyman Distillery – *journeymandistillery.com*

Mississippi River Distilling – *mrdistilling.com*

New Holland Artisan Spirits – *newhollandbrew.com*

Oregon Spirit Distillers – *oregonspiritdistillers.com*

Ozark Distillery – *ozarkdistillery.com*

Peach Street Distillers – *peachstreetdistillers.com*

Silverback Distillery – *sbdistillery.com*

Syntax Spirits – *syntaxspirits.com*

Thumb Butte Distillery – *thumbbuttedistillery.com*

Woodstone Creek – *woodstonecreek.com*

Bourbon Mixology
Bourbon Cocktails from the Companies Featured in
Small Brand America V

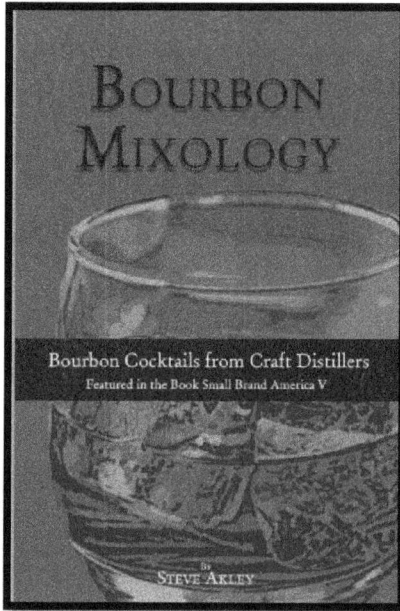

In this book, author Steve Akley took you behind the scenes of 20 craft distilleries making bourbon. Often, employees, fans, bartenders, distributors and even the company owners develop cocktail recipes to showcase their favorite distilled spirits. Steve assembled 50+ of the best bourbon cocktails from the companies featured in *Small Brand America V* and presents them in this new book titled: *Bourbon Mixology*.

The Importance of Online Reviews

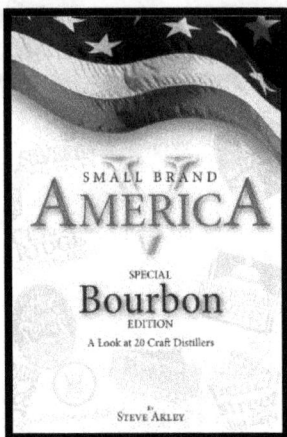

Reviews generate interest and create a buzz about the work of an author. Plus, your feedback is the only way an author knows if you enjoyed their work. Please take the time to review Small Brand America V! Steve would love to know what you think!

Bibliography/Sources

*In addition to the websites of the companies profiled (all listed in the **Author's Notes/Resources** section), the following resources were also utilized to create this book:*

Interview with 2bar Spirits Owner Nathan Kaiser: January 8, 2015.

Interview with 10th Mountain Whiskey & Spirit Company Founder Ryan Thompson: December 23, 2014.

Interview with Barrel House Distilling Co. Co-Owner Jeff Wiseman: January 15, 2015.

Interview with Black Dirt Distillery Co-Founder and Managing Partner Jeremy Kidde: January 6, 2015.

Interview with Cedar Ridge Vineyards General Manager Jamie Siefken: January 7, 2015.

Interview with Colorado Gold Distillery Head Distiller Mike Almy: December 23, 2014.

Interview with Coulter & Payne Farm Distillery Owner Chris Burnette: January 14, 2015.

Interview with Dark Corner Distillery Founder & President Joe Fenten: January 29, 2015.

Interview with Grand Traverse Distillery Owner Kent Rabish: January 27, 2015.

Interview with Heritage Distilling Co. CEO, Master Distiller and Founder Justin Stiefel: December 18, 2014.

Interview with Journeyman Distillery Office Manager Daniel Milsk: December 23, 2014.

Interview with Mississippi River Distilling Company Co-Owner Ryan Burchett: December 10, 2014.

Interview with New Holland Artisan Spirits Co-Founder and President Brett VanderKamp: December 16, 2014.

Interview with Oregon Spirit Distillers Owner Brad Irwin: January 22, 2014.

Interview with Ozark Distillery Head Distiller Dave Huffman: December 22, 2014.

Interview with Peach Tree Distillers Owner Rory Donovan: December 23, 2014.

Interview with Silverback Distillery CEO Christine Riggleman: December 9, 2014.

Interview with Syntax Spirits Co-Founder Heather Bean: December 15, 2014.

Interview with Thumb Butte Distillery Owner Dana Murdock: January 13, 2015.

Interview with Woodstone Creek Winery and Distillery Co-Owner Don Outterson: December 7, 2014.

Photographs

All photographs, in the sections of each business featured, have been utilized with permission from the respective companies with the following exceptions:

10th Mountain Spirit and Whiskey Company
In front of the still, Cups on the bar, Barrels lined up and Outside of the tasting room (Janie Viehman Photography)

Journeyman Distillery
The bar in the tasting room and Whiskey aging kit (Daniel Milsk)

Syntax Spirits
Heather bottle (Megan Verlee) and Wonder Woman (Eric Bellamy)

Woodstone Creek Artisan Winery and Distillery
Woodstone Bourbon updated look (*Cincinnati Magazine*)

Special Thanks

To my mom, Sandy Akley, and my wife Amy Akley, for their help in editing this book.

Thanks to my daughter Cat for just being herself.

Hats off to Mark Hansen (*mappersmark@gmail.com*) for the great cover design. He's the greatest graphic artist you will ever find!

The following individuals from the featured companies not only couldn't have been nicer, without their help this book would not have been possible:

Mike Almy, Colorado Gold Distillery

Heather Bean, Syntax Spirits

Brenda at *tnwhiskeychicks.com*

Chris Burnette, Coulter & Payne Farm Distillery

Ryan Burchett, Mississippi River Distilling Company

Rory Donovan, Peach Tree Distillers

Robert Downing, Barrel House Distilling Co.

Joe Fenten, Dark Corner Distillery

Tim Grovenburg, Dark Corner Distillery

Emily Haines, New Holland Artisan Spirits

Hannah Hanley, Heritage Distilling Co.

Perry Harmon, Grand Traverse Distillery

Scott Holderness, Thumb Butte Distillery

Dave Huffman, Ozark Distillery

Kathy & Brad Irwin, Oregon Spirit Distillers

Jeremy Kidde, Black Dirt Distillery

Daniel Milsk, Journeyman Distillery

Dana Murdock, Thumb Butte Distillery

Nathan Kaiser, 2bar Spirits

Don & Linda Outterson, Woodstone Creek Winery and Distillery

Louise Owens (Queen of All Things Divine Between NY and LA), Windmill Lounge (*windmill-lounge.com*/Dallas,TX)

Christine Riggleman, Silverback Distillery

Jamie Siefken, Cedar Ridge Vineyards

Justin Stiefel, Heritage Distilling Co.

Maddie Swanson, 2bar Spirits

Ryan Thompason, 10th Mountain Whiskey & Spirit Company

Brett VanderKamp, New Holland Artisan Spirits

Jeff Wiseman, Barrel House Distilling Co.

Lastly, lots of love for my father, Larry Akley. He's always with us in spirit.

In Loving Memory of Larry Akley
1942 – 2012

Dad's badge photo compliments of Kelly Brooks (thanks sis!)

Love A Cat Charity – Honolulu, Hawai'i

Steve Akley proudly supports the mission of Love A Cat Charity with a donation from the proceeds of the sale of all of his books.

Mission Statement

Love A Cat Charity's mission is to help end euthanasia of unwanted cats by caring for feral and abandoned felines, spaying or neutering them and, when appropriate, adopting them out. Love A Cat Charity emphasizes the use of Trap-Neuter-Return (TNR) technique to humanely control feral cat populations. Cats are humanely trapped, spayed or neutered and returned to their outdoor homes. TNR improves the cats' health and stabilizes the colony while allowing them to live out their lives outdoors. No new kittens are born and the cats no longer experience the stresses of mating and pregnancy.

Support of Love A Cat Charity in Honolulu, HI, helps cats like this sweet kitty

Love A Cat Charity
P.O. Box 11753
Honolulu, HI 96828
loveacatcharity.org

About the Author

Steve Akley is a lifelong St. Louis resident. Steve's approach to his writing is very simple. He knows his passion for writing comes from topics he enjoys so he sticks to what he knows best.

And yes... he likes bourbon:

Sign up for his newsletter, or check out his latest work, on his website: steveakley.com. Steve also maintains an author's page on Amazon.com. Just search his name on the site.

He can be reached via email: info@steveakley.com.

Find Steve on Social Media

 @steveakley WORDPRESS & Steve Akley

Small Brand America – The Series

This "Special Bourbon Edition" is the fifth edition and sixth overall book in Steve's *Small Brand America* series.

All Small Brand America books tell the stories of small companies taking on much larger competitors. You learn about the brands and the people behind them.

Here's a look at all of the books:

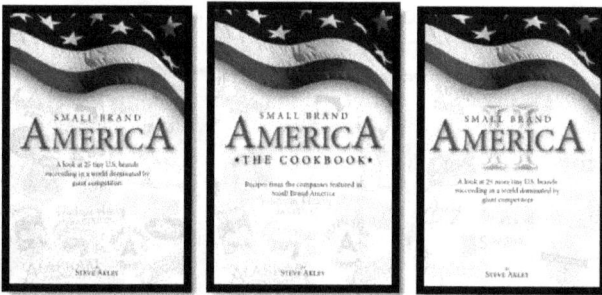

Small Brand America I & II each focus on 25 companies in the grocery business. Additionally, **Small Brand America I** has a companion piece; a cookbook featuring recipes from the companies highlighted in the book.

Small Brand America III & IV are each special editions. **SBA III** features companies all based in Hawaii and **SBA IV** features craft brewers.

Also by Steve Akley

Leo the Coffee Drinking Cat Series

A children's series featuring the adventures of a coffee drinking cat named Leo and his family.

Coffeehouse Jazz

Designed to assist you in building the ultimate playlists of jazz music. At 99¢, they cost less than the price of downloading a single song!

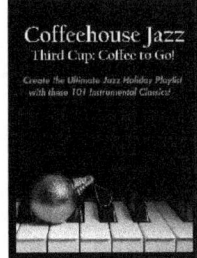

Steve Akley's Commuter Series

Short stories available for Kindle, iBooks and other electronic retailers

Only $1.49 each!

Be sure to check out Steve's website:

www.steveakley.com